MONSIEUR PROUST'S *LIBRARY*

also by AnKa

Balzac's Omelette:
A Delicious Tour of French Food
and Culture with Honoré de Balzac

Venice for Lovers
coauthored with Louis Begley

Elizabeth I and Mary Stuart:
The Perils of Marriage

A Passion for Freedom:
The Life of Astolphe de Custine

La Salle: Explorer of
the North American Frontier

Baron James: The Rise of
the French Rothschilds

MONSIEUR PROUST'S LIBRARY

ANKA MUHLSTEIN

OTHER PRESS

NEW YORK

Copyright © 2012 Anka Muhlstein
Due to limitations of space, acknowledgments for
permission to reprint previously published material
can be found on page 133.

Illustrations by Andreas Gurewich and Gary Roar.

Production Editor: Yvonne E. Cárdenas
Text Designer: Cassandra J. Pappas
This book was set in 10.75 pt Bodoni Book by
Alpha Design & Composition of Pittsfield, NH.

10 9 8 7 6 5 4 3 2 1

Library of Congress Cataloging-in-Publication Data
Muhlstein, Anka.
 Monsieur Proust's library / Anka Muhlstein.
  p. cm.
 Includes bibliographical references.
 ISBN 978-1-59051-566-2 (hardcover : acid-free paper)
— ISBN 978-1-59051-567-9 (ebook) 1. Proust, Marcel,
1871–1922—Books and reading. 2. Proust, Marcel,
1871–1922—Characters. I. Title.
 PQ2631.R63Z78925 2012
 843'.912—dc23   2012021629

to Helen Marx,
in memoriam

Table of CONTENTS

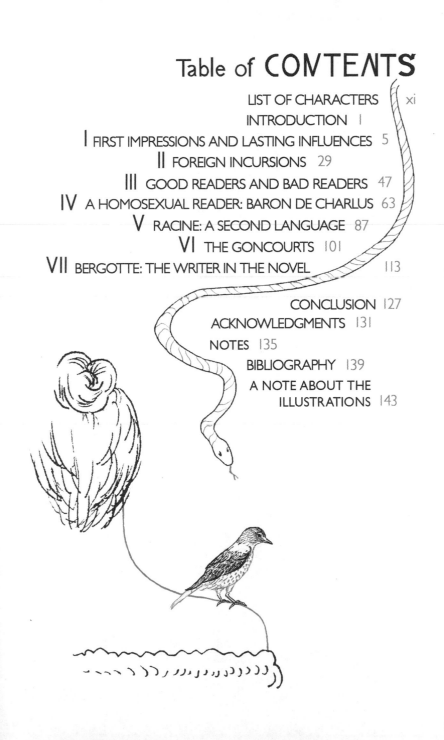

list of Characters

À la recherche du temps perdu, known as *In Search of Lost Time* in English, is a novel divided into seven books: *Swann's Way, Within a Budding Grove, The Guermantes Way, Sodom and Gomorrah, The Captive, The Fugitive,* and *Time Regained.* I will refer to the novel as a whole either simply as the Novel or by the truncated French title *La Recherche.*

The volume and page numbers standing alone in roman type in the footnotes refer to the English text of the four-volume Everyman's Library edition. The italicized references are to the three-volume French edition published by Robert Laffont in 1987.

I mention many characters from *In Search of Lost Time,* and some may not be familiar to every reader. The short list that follows is intended to help identify them.

The Narrator has no surname; only twice in the novel is he referred to as Marcel. When I speak of Marcel, I mean the Narrator, and "Proust" is a reference to the author.

The Narrator's family includes the mother; the father; the grandfather; the grandmother; Aunt Léonie, a permanent invalid who lives in the family house in the little town of Combray; two great-aunts, sisters of the grandmother; and Françoise, the family's cook.

The Guermantes family, the epitome of aristocratic grandeur, includes Basin, the Duke de Guermantes; Oriane, the Duchess de Guermantes; Palamède, Baron de Charlus, the Duke's brother; the Prince de Guermantes, the Duke's cousin; Mme de Villeparisis, the Duke's aunt; and Robert, Marquis de Saint-Loup, the Duke's nephew.

Albertine Simonet is the young girl the Narrator falls in love with in Balbec, a summer resort in Normandy. She comes to live with him in Paris. His possessiveness and insane jealousy will drive her to flee from his control.

Bergotte, an admirable writer, is one of the three great artists in the novel, the others being Elstir the painter and Vinteuil the composer.

Nissim Bernard, a successful Jewish businessman, is the uncle of Albert Bloch. He is described as a comical old homosexual queen, obsessed by young men.

Bloch is a schoolmate of the Narrator, with very strong literary opinions and terrible manners.

Brichot, a professor at the University of the Sorbonne, is a pedant, obsessed by etymology.

Baron de Charlus, the younger brother of the Duke de Guermantes, is a brilliant and strange man whose homosexuality is revealed in the course of the novel.

Françoise, the cook, moves to Paris with the Narrator's family after the death of Aunt Léonie and becomes the Narrator's testy factotum.

Jupien is a vest maker. He is completely devoted to Baron de Charlus and does his best to satisfy all his fantasies. He finally abandons his trade and becomes, thanks to the Baron, the owner of a male brothel.

Legrandin is a country neighbor, a rabid and very well-read snob.

Charles Morel, a gifted violinist but corrupt and cowardly, submits willingly to Baron de Charlus's protection, though he is himself attracted to women. He breaks with Charlus after a violent scene orchestrated by Mme Verdurin.

Marquis de Norpois, retired ambassador, friend of the Narrator's father and Mme de Villeparisis's lover.

Robert, Marquis de Saint-Loup, the Narrator's best friend, is in love with Rachel, a Jewish actress, but ultimately marries Gilberte Swann.

Charles Swann, the son of a Jewish stockbroker, is an old family friend and country neighbor of the Narrator's family, and also an intimate of the Guermantes. A great amateur of the arts, his knowledge of literature, painting, and music is recognized by all. He marries Odette de Crécy, a lady of very doubtful reputation, after a long and tumultuous affair. They have a child, Gilberte.

Marquis de Vaugoubert, ambassador to the fictional court of King Théodose.

M. and Mme Verdurin are the hosts of an artistic salon. Mme Verdurin, "the boss," reigns over it with an iron hand and excludes with decisive cruelty anyone she suspects of independence. They have mastered the art of hiding their social ambition.

Vinteuil, a great composer who leads such a modest and retired life in Combray that none of his neighbors and acquaintances are aware of his genius. He has a lesbian daughter who is always referred to as Mlle Vinteuil.

MONSIEUR
PROUST'S
LIBRARY

INTRODUCTION

Whether they follow an established tradition or rebel against it, whether they are authors of classics or are considered innovators, rare are the writers who were not also great readers. Proust was no exception to this rule; reading had always been his earliest and most important source of pleasure and stimulation, and it remained such. He is distinguished from his colleagues, however, by the immense role that literature plays in his oeuvre.

Proust seemed incapable of creating a character without putting a book in his hands. Two hundred characters inhabit the world he imagined, and some sixty writers preside over it. Certain of them, like Chateaubriand and Baudelaire, inspired him, while others, Mme de Sévigné, Racine, Saint-Simon, and Balzac, enhance his personages. Finally, Proust was so steeped in the works of his favorite authors that he gave characters they had created an important place in his own novel. Thus Racine's Phèdre plays an important role in the life of the Narrator, and Charlus would not be himself without Balzac's Vautrin.

There are as many ways of approaching a novel as complex as *La Recherche* as there are readers. The one I have chosen is to search through its subsoil and, in the process, shed light on subjects as varied as Proust's literary affinities, his passion for the classics, his curiosity about contemporary writers, and his knack of finding astonishingly apt quotations to put in the mouths of his characters.

Proust's friends claimed that he had read everything and forgot nothing. A book that undertook to provide a guide to Proust's great erudition would run the risk of being as long as *La Recherche*. I have narrowed my focus, and deal instead first with books to which he came early, those that turned him as a young boy into a passionate reader and enabled him to escape the narrow confines of a child's world, and, second, with the essential influence on *La Recherche* of Baudelaire and Ruskin, whose hidden, almost subterranean impact is often overlooked. Third, I devote attention to Racine and Balzac. Proust's reading of the tragedies of the former and the novels of the latter is so personal and distinctive that we may be bewildered at times to find their familiar characters or turns of phrase in unexpected contexts.

I

First impressions and lasting influences

How did Proust read? As a child, like all of us: for the plot and the characters. But even at a very young age reading was for him a very serious business, and he was outraged by the fact that it could be considered by grownups as something one did to amuse oneself. "My great-aunt," he recalled in *Days of Reading*, "would say to me, 'How can you go on amusing yourself with a book; it isn't Sunday, you know!' putting into the word 'amusing' an implication of childishness and waste of time."* For little Marcel Proust,

---

* Marcel Proust, *Days of Reading* (New York: Penguin Books, 2008), 77–78. Not in the Actes Sud edition of *Sur la Lecture*. Proust repeats this passage in *Swann's Way*. «*Comment tu t'amuses encore à lire, ce n'est pourtant pas dimanche*» *en donnant au mot amusement le sens d'enfantillage et de perte de temps*. Proust, *À la recherche du temps perdu* (Paris: Robert Laffont/Quid, 1987), *1:100* (hereafter cited by italicized volume and page number alone).

reading wasn't fun; it was traumatic. He cried at the end of every book and was unable to go to sleep, desolate at the idea of leaving the characters he had grown attached to: "these people for whom one has gasped or sobbed, one will know nothing more of them . . . one would have so liked for the book to continue."*

At the time, children didn't read books specifically written for young readers. They read renowned authors, generally in illustrated editions that were sometimes abridged. In Proust's case, both his grandmother and his mother gave him a lot of freedom to choose books and this family trait is reflected in the fictional family of *La Recherche*. The Narrator's grandmother was convinced that "light reading [was] as unwholesome as sweets and cakes, she did not reflect that the strong breath of genius might have upon the mind even of a child an influence at once more dangerous and less invigorating than that of fresh air and sea breezes upon his body."† In the novel, one evening, the young boy is so upset that his mother reluctantly agrees to spend the night in his room, and as he is too agitated to fall asleep, she reads to him *François le Champi* by George Sand, a somewhat curious choice.

The story is that of a foundling, an infant boy raised by Madeleine, a good woman married to a miller. The boy leaves

* Proust, *Days of Reading*, 63. *Ces gens pour qui on avait haleté ou sangloté on ne saurait plus rien d'eux. . . . On aurait tant voulu que le livre continuât.* Proust, *Sur la Lecture* (Paris: Actes Sud, 1988), 24–25.

† Proust, *In Search of Lost Time* (New York: Everyman's Library, Random House, 2001), 1:40 (hereafter cited by volume and page number alone). *Les lectures futiles [étaient] aussi malsaines que les bonbons et les pâtisseries, elle ne pensait pas que les grands souffles du génie eussent sur l'esprit même d'un enfant une influence plus dangereuse et moins vivifiante que sur son corps le grand air et le vent du large. 1:53.*

when he is old enough to find work, but returns to marry the widowed Madeleine, thus transforming a filial attachment into conjugal bliss. Marcel doesn't understand the plot—it doesn't help that his mother skips all the love scenes—but the strangeness adds to his pleasure. And although he will later comment on Sand's banality, and consider her work inferior to that of many of her contemporaries, the impression these first readings made on little Marcel, who in this instance as in others seems to inhabit the same body as the author, were profound. There is, however, a difference between them: the Narrator grows out of his fixation on his mother and falls in love with a series of girls, while Proust remained all his life passionately attached to his mother. That attachment may explain why he decided to use this story of a nearly incestuous relationship to illustrate the emotional state of his young hero.

At the very end of the novel, the Narrator suddenly sees *François le Champi* on a shelf in the Prince de Guermantes's library, and the mere sight of the volume triggers the memory of "the child I had been at that time, brought to life within me by the book, which knowing nothing of me except this child it had instantly summoned him to its presence, wanting to be seen only by his eyes, to be loved only by his heart, to speak only to him. And this book which my mother had read aloud to me at Combray until the early hours of the morning had kept for me all the charm of that night . . . [A] thousand trifling details of Combray which for years had not entered my mind came lightly and spontaneously leaping, in follow-my-leader fashion, to suspend themselves from the magnetised nib in an interminable and trembling chain of memories . . . [and re-created] the same impression of what the weather was like then in the garden, the same dreams that were then shaping themselves in [my] mind about the different countries and about life, the same anguish about the next day."* George Sand is the only writer Proust read as a child whom he comments upon in *La Recherche*, but he quotes many others in his letters to his mother and his grandmother, as he does in his first novel, *Jean Santeuil*, which he chose not to publish.

Young Proust was an enthusiastic reader. He adored, as many children did, Théophile Gautier's *Capitaine Fracasse*, a cloak-and-dagger story set in the seventeenth century, under the reign of Louis XIII. He loved the story's rhythm, the dialogue, the funny mention of Shakespeare as a "well-known English poet," and the fact that the author intervened openly in the narrative because, as he said in *Jean Santeuil*, "an author we love becomes a sort of oracle whom we like to consult on everything."[1] As we know, Proust himself often interjects authorial comments in his own *La Recherche*. Another family favorite was Alexandre Dumas, whom he quoted often in letters to his mother and to his brother, and continued to read for fun all his life.

---

* 4:453–55. *C'était l'enfant que j'étais alors, que le livre venait de susciter en moi, car de moi ne connaissant que cet enfant, c'est cet enfant que le livre avait appelé tout de suite, ne voulant être regardé que par ses yeux, aimé que par son cœur et ne parler qu'à lui. Aussi ce livre que ma mère m'avait lu à haute voix à Combray presque jusqu'au matin avait-il gardé pour moi tout le charme de cette nuit-là . . . Mille riens de Combray, et que je n'apercevais plus depuis longtemps, sautaient légèrement d'eux-mêmes et venaient à la queue-leu leu se suspendre au bec aimanté, en une chaîne interminable et tremblante de souvenirs [et recréait] la même impression du temps qu'il faisait dans le jardin, les mêmes rêves [que je formais] alors sur les pays et sur la vie, la même angoisse du lendemain. 3:716.*

How else would one read Dumas? "I like novels with no love stories, no dark passions but a lot of duels, policemen, kings and queens, good humor, and in which the innocents finish first."[*] And à propos of another Dumas novel, *Harmental*, he regretted that some twists and turns in the plot were going to bring about "painful conflicts in a novel in which I would have liked to find only happy curiosity, triumph, and gourmandise."[†]

But even as a child, Proust did serious reading, encouraged by his grandmother. He wrote to her how sad and beautiful he had found Balzac's *Eugénie Grandet*, and in the same letter incorporated quotes of Corneille, Racine, and Molière with abandon, perhaps to impress her with a familiarity—unusual for a teenager—with the classics. Later, in writing *La Recherche*, he will bring to perfection the skill of quoting and distorting the meaning of the quotes. At another time, he parodies a Homeric style by adding epithets to the immortal gods and goddesses he mentions, invoking for instance Pluto of the burning eyes and Artemis of the unblemished skin (a tic he will give many years later in his novel to Bloch, the pedantic young intellectual). Marcel recalls in *La Recherche* that he used to read Augustin Thierry, a historian of the Middle Ages, before setting off for a walk toward Méséglise. In real life,

* My translation. *J'aime [les romans] où il n'y a pas d'amour, ni de passions sombres, surtout des coups d'épée, de la police à la Chicot, de la royauté, de la bonne humeur et de la victoire des Innocents.* Proust, *Lettres à Reynaldo Hahn*, (Paris: Gallimard, 1956), 61.

† My translation. *des conflits douloureux dans un roman où je n'aurais voulu que de la curiosité heureuse, du triomphe et de la gourmandise.* Ibid., 114.

Proust reminded his mother how happy he had been long ago in Illiers, the little town in Normandy that he refashioned as Combray in the novel, where the family used to spend vacations, during the year when he was so taken by the works of Augustin Thierry. Very much influenced by the Romantics, Thierry evoked the past in a manner which could appeal well to a young reader. Proust called upon the memory of these readings in his description of Combray, where the past, and more precisely the Middle Ages, seems so vivid to the Narrator as a child. One of the reasons is that he is obsessed with the images of the Merovingian princess Geneviève de Brabant projected on the wall of his room by the magic lantern, set over his bed lamp, and given to him to distract him from his anxiety.[2] The other is that, when he is at mass, he is dazzled by the vibrancy of the stained glass windows of the church, which depict the descendants of Geneviève. He delights in the medieval aura in which the little town bathes. And he notices in the speech and the attitudes of the peasants and artisans who live in it a respect for traditions that have come down "unbroken, oral, distorted, unrecognisable, and alive"* from past centuries. The first time the child sees Françoise, his aunt's cook, "beneath the frills of a snowy bonnet as stiff and fragile as if it had been made of spun sugar," he thinks she looks like "a saint in her niche."† When he gets to know her better, he is struck by the fact that she incorporates completely the distant past in her

* 1:149. *une tradition ininterrompue, orale, déformée, méconnaissable et vivante. 1:139.*

† 1:53. *sous les tuyaux d'un bonnet éblouissant, raide et fragile comme s'il avait été de sucre filé . . . comme une statue de sainte dans sa niche. 1:63.*

way of thinking: in her kitchen, she holds "forth about Saint Louis [who died during his second Crusade in 1270] as though she herself had known him, generally in order to depreciate, by contrast with him, my grandparents whom she considered less 'righteous.'"* When the Narrator comes to Combray, the link between the distant past and the present becomes specific and concrete, as the local priest explains to him that the direct ancestors of the Duke and Duchess de Guermantes, the Abbots of Combray, and Lords of Guermantes, are buried in the village church.

The Narrator and Proust, unsurprisingly, were attached to the same books in their childhood. This is one of the instances where the reader may be justified in identifying the author with the character. Proust said over and over again that *La Recherche* was not autobiographical, and one should indeed resist the temptation of confusing him with the "I" of the book. Nevertheless, when it comes to literary and artistic matters, they obviously overlap.

In the same scene I have mentioned in the Prince de Guermantes's library, as the Narrator admires the beautiful bindings of the Prince's books, he reflects that if he himself had been a bibliophile, the "first edition of a work would have been more precious in my eyes than any other, but by this term I should have understood the edition in which I read it for the first time. I should seek out original editions, those, that is to say, in which I once received an original impression of a book. For the impressions that one has later are no longer

* 1:148. *Françoise à la cuisine parlait volontiers de Saint Louis, comme si elle l'avait personnellement connu, et généralement pour faire honte par la comparaison à mes grands-parents moins «justes». 1:139.*

original. In the case of novels I should collect old-fashioned bindings, those of the period when I read my first novels, those that so often heard Papa say to me: 'Sit up straight!'"*

As a schoolboy, Proust read more contemporary and foreign literature than most of his friends. Probable reasons were the asthma attacks that often obliged him to skip classes, giving him more time for reading, as well as his complete lack of interest in mathematics. ("Does absolutely nothing," commented his math teacher in a report card.) His favorite subjects were the natural sciences, history, and, of course, literature. By the time he was in *seconde*, the equivalent of tenth grade, he had discovered both Anatole France's ironical, skeptical, and often racy novels written in the purest French and those of Pierre Loti, whose style is very sensual and impressionistic; he was familiar with the obscure poetry of Stéphane Mallarmé, and memorized poems by Leconte de Lisle, holding in high regard his detachment, precision, and richness of classical references. And Proust had read a number of novels by Dostoyevsky, Tolstoy, Dickens, and George Eliot.

As he grew older, he also became more attuned to the formal beauty of texts; he read the old masters—especially Racine and Saint-Simon—not only for the intellectual and emotional impact of their work but also for their use of language: "Something of the happiness one feels taking a

* 4:456. *La première édition d'un ouvrage m'eût été plus précieuse que les autres, mais j'aurais entendu par elle l'édition où je le lus pour la première fois. Je recherchais les éditions originales, je veux dire celles où j'eus de ce livre une impression originale. Car les impressions suivantes ne le sont plus. Je collectionnerais pour les romans les reliures d'autrefois, celles du temps où je lus mes premiers romans et qui entendaient Papa me dire «Tiens-toi droit». 3:718.*

walk in a city like Beaune, that has preserved intact its fif-
teenth century hospital, one can feel again wandering in the
midst of a tragedy by Racine or a volume of Saint-Simon."[*]
The syntax and the vocabulary of the seventeenth century
evoked customs and ways of thinking that had disappeared
and had the poetic charm of times gone by. Of course, this
feeling of nostalgia was only one element, and perhaps not
the most important one, of his passion for the literature of
the classical era. Even before appreciating the depth and
complexity of Racine's analysis of love and jealousy, before
the drama of the court of Louis XIV depicted by the Duke
de Saint-Simon, a memoirist of unrivaled brilliance, had en-
grossed him, he already treasured and attempted to absorb
the original style of these masters and learned from them.
From the bewildering embroideries that he compared to the
suckers that appear after the flowering of a plant, character-
istic of Saint-Simon's sentences, he learned the importance
of being unpredictable to his reader. Like the memoirist,
he feared not being able to express all his thoughts or feelings. Both Saint-Simon, scribbling away in his closet-sized
office in the wee hours of the night (he spent his days passionately observing the goings-on at Versailles), and Proust
in his bed, struggling to finish his novel before he died, had
the feeling they had too much to say and too little time to do
it. "I am carried away by my subject," wrote Saint-Simon, a
sentiment echoed by Proust: he had so much to say that he

* Proust, *Days of Reading*, 50. *Un peu du bonheur qu'on éprouve à se promener
dans une ville comme Beaune qui garde intact son hôpital du XVème siècle [on
le ressent encore] à errer au milieu d'une tragédie de Racine ou d'un volume de
Saint-Simon.* Proust, *Sur la Lecture*, 50–51.

felt ideas coming at him "like crashing waves."* In Saint-Simon, this feeling of urgency results in violent oppositions, audacious comparisons, or the heaping one upon another of contrasting images; in Proust in endless meanders, twists, and turns. The Duke knew perfectly that he was often transgressing the rules of accepted usage but was not fazed. He declared proudly: *Je ne fus jamais un sujet académique.*[3] This disdain for ordinary rules of grammar sacrificed in order to obtain more strength in expression was also to be found in Racine, and Proust wrote admiringly of his daring elisions at the expense of what was considered correct usage. He gives an example taken from *Andromaque*: Hermione asks Oreste to kill Pyrrhus to avenge his having scorned her. She instantly regrets her words but, before she can stop the murder, Oreste appears and announces that Pyrrhus is dead. Why? rages Hermione:

Pourquoi l'assassiner? Qu'a-t-il fait? A quel titre?
Qui te l'a dit?

"Why kill him? What did he do? On what grounds? Who told you?" One should note here that Anglophones do not adhere with as much rigidity to the rules of language and syntax as the French do, so Hermione's desperate screams do not strike them as ungrammatical. For a reader who is the product of a French lycée, and who is used to the corseted rhythms of alexandrine verses, both the staccato pulse of the speech and the progression can be startling. He would expect

* My translation. *Cela se presse comme des flots,* quoted by Jean Mouton, *Le Style de Marcel Proust* (Paris: Éditions Corréa, 1948), 61.

to go from what had he done, to why kill him, to who told you to do it, and, finally to by what right was the order given. However, for a sensitive reader steeped in French classics, Racine's ordering of Hermione's speech, his bold omissions and grammatical incorrectness, is vastly more powerful. It shows that Hermione's reason has been unmoored by wild despair. Even the clarity of meaning, so prized by the French, is missing here. Hermione's last question, Who told you? reveals even in English a certain ambiguity: Does she mean Who told you about it? or Who told you to do it?

This forceful twisting of ordinary rules is, of course, what attracted Proust to Racine. He appreciated that Racine knew that the only way to defend the language was to attack it, and to submit to its perpetual and dizzyingly swift changes. Proust pressed this point, writing that "Racine's most famous lines have become celebrated because they can produce this sense of delight by reason of a familiar piece of linguistic daring which stands like a bold bridge spawning two gentle banks."* He was quite convinced, as he wrote to his friend Mme Straus, that, ironically, no contemporary editor would permit such liberties.[4] These were lessons Proust would never forget. Already as a schoolboy, encouraged by one of his beloved teachers, M. Darlu, who set a high value on true originality, he began to cultivate a decidedly personal style.

Very early, Proust became convinced that one could develop a distinctive voice and style only through being true

* My translation. *Les plus célèbres vers de Racine le sont en réalité parce qu'ils charment ainsi par quelque audace familière de langage jeté comme un pont hardi entre deux rives de douceur. Sésame et les Lys*, quoted by René de Chantal, *Marcel Proust, critique littéraire* (Montréal: Presses de l'Université de Montréal, 1967), 1:354.

to one's *réalité intérieure*. Inspired by Saint-Simon and by Racine, he asserted that "each writer is bound to create his own language as each violinist must create his own 'tone.' This idea that there is a French language that exists outside of the writers who use it and that must be protected is fantastic."[*]

Proust's habit of reading as an artisan of the written word, endlessly analyzing the style and technique of other authors, whether he liked their work or not, was one he acquired at school and did not abandon when he began writing in earnest. Because imitation came to him so naturally, the intimate sense of an author's style that he was able to acquire involved certain risks. He felt particularly vulnerable because his ear, which he called his inner metronome, was keenly attuned to rhythms of speech. As he once told a friend, once you have the tune, the words come easily. This is why he would cleanse himself, as he put it, by writing pastiches—it was his way to get the rhythms of Balzac or Flaubert and their idiosyncrasies out of his system. Proust published his many pastiches separately. However, he allowed some of his characters to express themselves in a way that immediately brought to mind the mannerisms of a well-known author. For instance, Anatole France's preciousness can be detected in the speech of M. Legrandin, the morbidly snobbish country neighbor of the Narrator's family, and France's style in the writing Proust

* Proust, *Letters of Marcel Proust*, trans. Mina Curtiss (New York: Helen Marx Books, 2006), 216. *Chaque écrivain est obligé de faire sa langue, comme chaque violoniste est obligé de faire son «son». Cette idée qu'il y une langue française, existant en dehors des écrivains, et qu'on protège est inouïe.* Proust, *Lettres* (Paris: Éditions Plon, 2004), 461.

attributes to Bergotte, the fictional writer in *La Recherche.* And he incorporated in the novel a great spoof of the Goncourt brothers' journal when he has the Narrator, staying in the country with Gilberte Swann, pick up their latest volume.

Proust considered that an original writer was entitled to stray from strict rules of syntax but was bound to respect scrupulously the precise meanings of words. He admits that names of cities, for instance Parma or Florence, so inflame the imagination they transcend the geopolitical reality. For the Narrator to live in Parma would be to live in a "compact, smooth, violet-tinted and soft"[*] house, a conception due not to anything real but to the reading of Stendhal's *Charterhouse of Parma* and the evocation of violets. But common words should be used with the utmost exactitude. "Words present to us a little picture of things, clear and familiar, like the pictures hung on the walls of school-rooms to give children an illustration of what is meant by a carpenter's bench, a bird, an anthill, things chosen as typical of everything else of the same sort."[†] And in that perspective, he gives his due to Victor Hugo. If challenged, Hugo was able to defend his use of a word: he could "establish its filiation, right back to its origin, with citations that were proof of genuine erudition. . . . A great writer should have in-depth

---

[*] 1:378. *Lisse, compacte, mauve et douce. 1:320.*

[†] 1:378. *Les mots nous présentent des choses une petite image claire et usuelle comme celles que l'on suspend aux murs des écoles pour donner aux enfants l'exemple de ce qu'est un établi, un oiseau, une fourmilière, choses conçues comme pareilles à toutes celles d'une même sorte. 1:320.*

knowledge of his dictionary and be able to follow a word through the ages in the works of all great writers who have used it."*

Style preoccupied Proust greatly, but memory, and particularly the phenomenon of involuntary memory and its potential role in artistic creation, obsessed him. Three writers, François de Chateaubriand, Gérard de Nerval, and Charles Baudelaire, shared this obsession. Chateaubriand was of the generation of men who had lived through the Revolution, the Napoleonic era, and the return of the monarchy; the two poets, Nerval and Baudelaire, were born at the beginning of the nineteenth century. Chateaubriand is best known for his memoirs, published after his death, hence their title, *Memoirs from Beyond the Grave*. Even if these predecessors had not shown Proust the way, they gave him, or more precisely the Narrator, the certainty that he was on the right path. The best-known passage in *La Recherche* is doubtless the episode of the madeleine, in which the Narrator describes how the seemingly long-forgotten taste of the little cake soaked in hot tea brought back his childhood memories. Chateaubriand had used this technique, but, in his case, it was a sound that awakened the involuntary memory. Proust recognized the debt to his predecessor for a process that would prove all-important in *La Recherche* in a candid admission: "And

* Adriana Hunter's translation. *en établir la filiation, jusqu'à l'origine, par des citations qui prouvaient une véritable érudition . . . Un grand écrivain doit savoir à fond son dictionnaire et pouvoir suivre un mot à travers les âges chez tous les grands écrivains qui l'ont employé.* Proust, *Pastiches et mélanges*, in *Contre Sainte-Beuve* (Paris: Gallimard, 1971), 184 and 806.

in one of the masterpieces of French literature . . . the *Mémoires d'outre-tombe* . . . there figures a sensation of the same species as the taste of the madeleine."* And he quotes the passage: "Yesterday evening I was walking alone . . . I was roused from my reflexions by the warbling of a thrush perched upon the highest branch of a birch-tree. Instantaneously the magic sound caused my father's estate to reappear before my eyes . . . I saw again those country scenes in which I had so often heard the fluting notes of the thrush."[5] The Narrator goes on to quote Nerval and Baudelaire, who had also explored these instances of involuntary memory sparked by transient sensations, and admits his pride in being able "to establish my place in so noble a line of descent and thus to give myself the assurance that the work which I no longer had any hesitation in undertaking was worthy of the pains which I should have to bestow upon it."†

That Baudelaire's impact may be detected in other ways is not surprising. Of his preferred nineteenth-century poets— the others were Vigny, Nerval, and Hugo—Baudelaire was the one Proust read with the greatest passion. He declared in a long letter to a lady with literary tastes, Mme Fortoul, whom he had met on a boating expedition, that "Baudelaire [was] one of the poets [he liked] the best and about whose

* 4:488–89. *N'est-ce-pas à mes sensations du genre de celle de la madeleine qu'est suspendue la plus belle partie des Mémoires d'outre-tombe? 3:744.*

† 4:489. *Dans une filiation aussi noble, et me donner par là l'assurance que l'œuvre que je n'aurais plus aucune hésitation à entreprendre méritait l'effort que j'allais lui consacrer. 3:744.*

life and bibliography [he knew] the least"[6] and with whom he had the most affinities. He may have indeed imagined he was the reader Baudelaire had in mind when the poet addressed his work to a *Hypocrite lecteur, mon semblable, mon frère.* Critics have often commented on the similarities between the two men, who both remained absorbed by the lost paradise of their childhood, were passionately attached to their mothers, fell sick at a relatively young age, and used narcotics freely. More important, Proust recognized in Baudelaire the lack of determination from which he too suffered, which had for many years paralyzed his as well as Baudelaire's creative force, and admired the juxtaposition of cruelty and hidden tenderness in certain poems, the sudden changes of pace, and the striking and often jarring originality of Baudelaire's images. He responded strongly to the latent homosexuality he perceived in the poet, as well as to his interest in lesbianism evident in "Lesbos" and "Femmes damnées."

As we know, Proust started *La Recherche* in earnest only in his late thirties. Although he had written many articles, an unfinished novel, and thousands of notes, he continued to be anguished by a seeming inability to find a satisfying form for the new work and then to make the necessary effort to conclude it. The thought of Baudelaire's hesitations, which Proust ascribed to laziness, doubts, and even lack of power, did not in his mind excuse his own shortcomings, but it brought a degree of comfort: "Should I write a novel? A philosophical essay? Am I a novelist? I find it consoling that Baudelaire based his *Petits Poèmes en prose* and *Les*

Fleurs du Mal on the same subject."[7] Proust perceived in these hesitations over the form to adopt a lack of willpower or of artistic instinct but also the "predominance of intelligence which is more inclined to point out all the different paths than to choose any one."[*] Proust was also extremely unsettled by critics who failed to see Baudelaire's immense sensitivity in his evocations of the worst sufferings, in his cruel and precise descriptions of the horrors of poverty, old age, sickness, and death. The poem on old women, "Les Petites Vieilles," was one to which Proust returned many times in *Contre Sainte-Beuve* to make his point:

> *In ragged skirts and threadbare finery*
> *They creep, tormented by the wicked gusts,*
> *Cowering each times an omnibus*
> *Thunders past, and clutching a reticule*
> *As if it were a relic sewn with spells.*
> *Whether they mince like marionettes or drag*
> *Themselves along like wounded animals*
> *They dance—against their will, the creatures dance—*
> *Sad bells on which a merciless Devil tugs.*[†]

* Adriana Hunter's translation. *prédominance de l'intelligence qui indique plutôt les voies différentes qu'elle ne passe en une.* Proust, *Contre Sainte-Beuve* (1954), 159.

† Richard Howard's translation. Baudelaire, *Les Fleurs du Mal* (Boston: Godine, 1983), 94. *Sous des jupons troués et sous de froids tissus/Ils rampent flagellés par les bises iniques/Frémissant au fracas roulant des omnibus/Et serrant sur leurs flancs ainsi que des reliques,/Un petit sac brodé de fleurs ou de rébus;/ Ils trottent, tout pareil à des marionnettes;/Se traînent, comme font les animaux blessés,/Ou dansent, sans vouloir danser, pauvres sonnettes/Où se pend un Démon sans pitié.* Baudelaire, *Tableaux parisiens*, in *Œuvres complètes* (Paris: Gallimard, 1975–76), 89.

It is in this deliberate refusal to be compassionate that Proust saw the best expression of Baudelaire's genius. "Perhaps this subordination of sensibility to truth and statement is ultimately a sign of genius, of the force of art overcoming a personal compassion."* There is a great scene in *La Recherche,* in which Proust displayed the same apparent lack of sensitivity: the death of the adored grandmother. The whole family is assembled around the deathbed, and Proust marks the varying attitudes among its different members. The mother "stood with the unheeding desolation of a tree lashed by the rain and shaken by the wind,"† while the men of the family were tiring of this long agony: "Their continuous devotion ended by assuming a mask of indifference, and their interminable enforced idleness around this deathbed made them indulge in the sort of small talk that is an inseparable accompaniment of prolonged confinement in a railway carriage."‡ The Narrator, for his part, is transfixed by the appearance of the dying woman: "Bent in a semi-circle on the bed, a creature other than my grandmother, a sort of beast that had put on her hair and crouched among her bedclothes, lay panting, whimpering, making the blankets heave with

---

* Proust, *By Way of Sainte-Beuve*, trans. Sylvia Townsend Warner (London: Chatto and Windus, 1958), 98. *Peut-être cette subordination de la sensibilité à la vérité, à l'expression, est-elle au fond une marque de génie, de la force de l'art supérieur à la pitié individuelle. Contre Sainte-Beuve (1971), 252.*

† 2:620. *avait la désolation sans pensée d'un feuillage que cingle la pluie et retourne le vent. 2:289.*

‡ 2:617. *Leur dévouement continu finissait pas prendre un masque d'indifférence, et l'interminable oisiveté autour de cette agonie leur faisait tenir les mêmes propos qui sont inséparables d'un séjour prolongé dans un wagon de chemin de fer. 2:289.*

its convulsions. The eyelids were closed, and it was because they did not shut properly rather than because they opened that they disclosed a chink of the eyeball, blurred, rheumy, reflecting the dimness of an organic vision and of an inward pain."[*] This vision is as cruel as anything in Baudelaire's work, and yet as Proust's readers, are we not convinced, just as was Proust when he read Baudelaire's most clinically cruel poems, that he like the poet has "experienced it all, understood it all, and has the most quivering sensibility and the profoundest comprehension?"[†] The curious switches of tone, often found in Baudelaire, attracted Proust's attention, and he pointed out the strange absence of transition in certain poems. It is a method Proust often used himself, but typically for comic effects. For instance, he interrupts the death scene by introducing the Duke de Guermantes, anxious to pay his respects to the mourning family; but the Duke's bewilderment at not being greeted with all the consideration and gratitude he considers his due brings about a complete change of atmosphere. One finds these shocking contrasts not only in dramatic scenes but also in descriptions and digressions. For instance, in a passage in which he discusses the different forms suffering takes in Baudelaire, he concludes with an

[*] 2:612. *Courbée en demi-cercle sur le lit, un autre être que ma grand'mère, une espèce de bête qui se serait affublée de ses cheveux et couchée dans ses draps, haletait, geignait, de ses convulsions secouait les couvertures. Les paupières étaient closes et c'est parce qu'elles fermaient mal plutôt que parce qu'elles s'ouvraient qu'elles laissaient voir un coin de prunelle, voilé, chassieux, reflétant l'obscurité d'une vision organique et d'une souffrance interne. 2:283.*

[†] Proust, *By Way of Sainte-Beuve*, 99. *[Le poète] a tout ressenti, tout compris, qu'il est la plus frémissante sensibilité, la plus profonde intelligence. Contre Sainte-Beuve* (1971), 253.

astonishing image: "Over each type of humankind, he puts one of these great phrases, all warm and supple, full of scent and sap, one of these bags that could hold a bottle of wine, or a ham."[*]

Like the other poets who captivated Proust, Baudelaire had a special hold on his imagination because of his conception of love, so particular, and often bizarre, and so different from, for instance, that of Victor Hugo. Most people do not think of Baudelaire as a homosexual: Proust's dissenting view was expressed in *Contre Sainte-Beuve*, in an article he wrote on Baudelaire, and in conversations with André Gide. He contrasts famous lines in Alfred de Vigny's "La Colère de Samson,"

Woman will have Gomorrah and Man will have Sodom
And casting an irritated look at one another from afar
The two sexes will die each on their own side[†]

inspired by Vigny's jealous and unhappy love for the actress Madame Dorval, who was attracted to women, with Baudelaire's vision in his poem "Lesbos," of a man seduced by the mysteries of Sapphic love:

[*] Ibid., 99. *Sur chaque catégorie de personne [Baudelaire] pose toute chaude et suave, pleine de liqueur et de parfum, une de ces grandes formes, de ces sacs qui pourraient contenir une bouteille ou un jambon. Contre Sainte-Beuve* (1971), 253.

[†] My translation. *La Femme aura Gomorrhe et l'Homme aura Sodome/ Et se jetant de loin un regard irrité/Les deux sexes mourront chacun de leur côté.* Alfred de Vigny, *Œuvres poétiques* (Paris: Garnier-Flammarion, 1978), 219.

For Lesbos has chosen me among all men
to sing the secret of her budding grove;
from childhood I have shared the mystery
*of frenzied laughter laced with sullen tears.**

Proust was convinced that Baudelaire was attracted to both sexes (curiously, he gave this quality in his novel to Charles Morel, the violinist who ensnares Baron de Charlus and is equally ready to bestow his sexual favors on men and on straight and lesbian women). He presented this theory to André Gide, to the latter's considerable astonishment. A very successful writer, Gide was the influential literary director of Les Éditions de la NRF—which later became Les Éditions Gallimard—and, as such, had been personally responsible for Gallimard's rejection of *Swann's Way* in 1912, an astounding mistake that he tried to explain in a long letter to Proust, hoping to be forgiven.[8] Proust did not hold a grudge; and although never close, the two men went on to have cordial relations. Gide was a homosexual, and one of the rare people with whom Proust is known to have had explicit conversations on the subject of sexual inversion. Gide recorded one of them, concerning Baudelaire, in his journal: "Proust tells me his conviction that Baudelaire was homosexual: 'The way he speaks of *Lesbos*, and the mere need of speaking of it, would be enough to convince

* Richard Howard's translation. Baudelaire, *Les Fleurs du Mal*, 125. *Car Lesbos entre tous m'a choisi sur la terre/Pour chanter le secret de ses vierges en fleurs/Et je fus dès l'enfance admis au noir mystère/Des rires effrénés mêlés aux sombres pleurs.* Baudelaire, *Œuvres complètes, 151.*

me,' and when I protest: 'In any case, if he was homosexual, it was almost without his knowing it, and you don't believe he ever practiced. . . .' 'What,' he exclaims. 'I am sure of the contrary; how can you doubt he practiced. He, Baudelaire!' And in the tone of his voice, it is implied that by doubting it, I am insulting Baudelaire.'"*

Baudelaire and Proust shared the same tragic conception of homosexuality as a curse. There is no reason to suppose that Baudelaire influenced Proust in this regard, but the affinity of the two visions is indisputable. In "Femmes damnées," Baudelaire writes:

Wandering far from all mankind, condemned
To forage in the wilderness like wolves,
Pursue your fate, chaotic souls, and flee
The infinite you bear within yourselves![†]

Proust, in *Sodom and Gomorrah*, laments the fate of men like Oscar Wilde: "Their honour precarious, their liberty provisional, lasting only until the discovery of their crime;

---

* André Gide, *Journals*, trans. Justin O'Brien (New York: Knopf, 1948), 2:265. *Proust me dit la conviction où il est que Baudelaire était un uraniste. «La manière dont il parle de Lesbos, et déjà le besoin d'en parler, suffiraient seuls à m'en convaincre» et comme je proteste en tout cas que s'il était uraniste, c'était à son insu puisque vous ne pouvez penser qu'il aît jamais pratiqué. Comment donc, s'écrit-il, je suis convaincu du contraire. Comment pouvez-vous douter qu'il pratiquât? lui, Baudelaire! Et dans le ton de sa voix, il semblait qu'en doutant, je fasse injure à Baudelaire.* Gide, *Journal 1887–1925* (Paris: Gallimard, 1996), entry dated May 14, 1921, 1124.

† Richard Howard's translation. Baudelaire, *Les Fleurs du Mal*, 129. *Loin des peuples vivants, errantes condamnées/A travers les déserts, courez comme les loups/Faites votre destin, âmes désordonnées/Et fuyez l'infini que vous portez en vous.* Baudelaire, *Œuvres complètes*, 155.

their position unstable like that of the poet one day fêted in every drawing-room and applauded in every theatre in London, and the next driven from every lodging, unable to find a pillow upon which to lay his head."[*]

Finally, no one understood better than Proust the meaning of the famous line from Baudelaire's poem "Correspondances," "The sounds, the scents, the colors correspond,"[†] and he echoed it in stunningly unexpected associations, whether he was writing about a city the name of which evokes butter, or of a fish that he imagines as a cathedral: "Coutances, a Norman cathedral which its final consonants, rich and yellowing, crowned with a tower of butter";[‡] "a fish whose body with its numberless vertebrae, its blue and pink veins, had been constructed by nature, but according to an architectural plan, like a polychrome cathedral of the deep."[§]

However, while Baron de Charlus, for instance, is inseparable from Saint-Simon, no character in *La Recherche* immediately brings to mind Baudelaire. Proust never *uses* the poet to create such an effect. Instead, he absorbed Baudelaire's

---

[*] 3:17. *Sans honneur que précaire, sans liberté que provisoire, jusqu'à la découverte du crime; sans situation qu'instable, comme pour le poète la veille fêté dans tous les salons, applaudi dans tous les théâtres de Londres, chassé le lendemain de tous les garnis sans pouvoir trouver un oreiller où reposer sa tête. 2:510.*

[†] Richard Howard's translation. Baudelaire, *Les Fleurs du Mal*, 15. *Les parfums, les couleurs et les sons se répondent.* Baudelaire, "Correspondances," in *Spleen et Idéal, Œuvres complètes, 11.*

[‡] 1:379. *Coutances que sa diphtongue finale, grasse et jaunissante couronne comme une motte de beurre 1:320.*

[§] 2:53. *Quelque vaste poisson, monstre marin, . . . et duquel le corps aux innombrables vertèbres, aux nerfs bleus et roses avait été construit par la nature, mais selon un plan architectural, comme une polychrome cathédrale de la mer. 1:573.*

work in a manner so deep and personal that Baudelaire's presence in the novel is inescapable yet hidden.

The writers who star in *La Recherche* are all French, and I shall return to them, but it is a mistake to disregard the strong influence on Proust of British literature. The fact that Ruskin, Stevenson, Eliot, and Hardy are rarely mentioned in the novel is not an indication of their lack of importance. Like Baudelaire, they have been completely interiorized. In a letter to the diplomat Robert de Billy, a college friend, he wrote: "It is curious that in all the different genres, from George Eliot to Hardy, from Stevenson to Emerson, there is no literature which has had as much hold on me as English and American literature. Germany, Italy, very often France leave me indifferent but two pages of *The Mill on the Floss* reduce me to tears."[9] Proust did not refer to Ruskin in the letter but his influence on Proust was greater than that of any other non-French writer. Named only four times in *La Recherche*, Ruskin's attenuated presence, which is more like an absence, illustrates perfectly the Narrator's quip: "a book is a huge cemetery in which on the majority of the tombs the names are effaced and can no longer be read."[*] Ruskin's monument towers in this imaginary necropolis.

---

[*] 4:472. *Un livre est un grand cimetière où sur la plupart des tombes on ne peut plus lire les noms effacés. 3:733.*

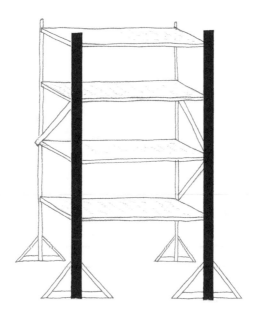

Foreign Incursions

In a French lycée, pupils specializing in humanities were required to study Latin, Greek, and one modern language. Proust chose German, a language his maternal grandmother had started to teach him two years before he entered the lycée at the age of eleven. One of the very first surviving letters of Marcel Proust is a five-line note in German addressed to her. However, German writers, apart from Goethe, never appealed to him. He went so far as to declare in 1915 that contemporary German literature was nonexistent. He was apparently unaware of Thomas Mann or for that matter Sigmund Freud. On the other hand, Russian and British literature attracted him considerably. And among English writers, none fascinated him more than John Ruskin.

John Ruskin was a hugely influential nineteenth-century art critic who wrote on a wide variety of subjects: architecture, sculpture, painting, and literature, as well as geology, botany, ornithology, education, and even political economy. Proust discovered him through a French art historian, Robert de la Sizeranne, author of a study on Ruskin, *Ruskin et la religion de la beauté*. His enthusiasm was kindled by Ruskin's conception of the artist as interpreter, a link between nature and men, and his belief that beauty resided in "the simplest of objects . . . [in] the most beloved sights that you see every summer evening along thousands of footpaths, the streams of water on the hillsides . . . of your old, familiar countryside."[1] That the artist should only paint or describe what he sees was a precept which delighted Proust, who claimed he had no imagination. In *La Recherche*, the painter Elstir will present this very same theory to the Narrator. He needs to shed all preconceptions when he starts a painting in order to paint only what he sees and not what he knows.

Proust spent nine years immersed in Ruskin. Ruskin was the only English writer he made the effort to read in the original, even though his knowledge of the language was flimsy. It is a pity that he didn't take English at his lycée. If he had, he might have been taught by none other than Stéphane Mallarmé, the poet he admired so deeply. His enthusiasm for Ruskin grew to the point that he abandoned the novel he was working on, *Jean Santeuil*—which remained unfinished and unpublished—to translate his works. He explained to a friend, Constantin de Brancovan, who wondered how he could translate from a language he did not know, that he had learned English while suffering from severe attacks of asthma. As I could not speak, Proust explained, I learned the language with my eyes. I do not know spoken English; I would not know how to ask for a glass of water because I do not know how to pronounce words or recognize them when they are pronounced. "I do not claim to know English," he concluded, "I claim to know Ruskin."* In fact, he learned entire volumes of Ruskin by heart, and was able to recite from memory all of Ruskin's *The Bible of Amiens*. The task of translating, he admitted, could not have been accomplished without the help of his mother. Completely fluent in English, she would write the first draft that he subsequently reworked. He also took advice from a few friends, among them a young Englishwoman, Marie Nordlinger, with whose cousin, the composer Reynaldo Hahn, he had had an obsessive love affair. By 1896, the passion for the young man had turned to a friendship that would endure until Proust's death. Proust started work on his Ruskin translation in 1899 and persevered for five years, notwithstanding moments of disenchantment and impatience. Without his mother's encouragement, the project might have been abandoned, but Proust was placing himself within an established literary tradition.

Great writers of the nineteenth and early twentieth century often undertook the task of translating their favorite authors. Chateaubriand tackled Milton, Hugo took on

---

* My translation. *Je ne prétends pas savoir l'anglais. Je prétends savoir Ruskin.* Marcel Proust to Constantin de Brancovan, n.d., in Proust, *Lettres*, 233.

Shakespeare, as did Gide, and Nerval devoted himself to both Goethe and Heine. Translating Ruskin was therefore anything but idiosyncratic; it was a partial shield against the accusation, which pained him, that he was a mere dilettante. It improved his work habits. When Ruskin died in 1900, Proust was asked by an art magazine, *La Chronique des Arts et de la Curiosité*, to write a long obituary. From then on he was recognized in France as an authority on the English master; a few months later he wrote two other articles on him in the very influential *Gazette des Beaux-Arts*.

His restlessness, however, had been very real. He confessed in 1904 to Marie Nordlinger that the old man was beginning to bore him. In a 1908 letter to the novelist George de Lauris, one of the few friends who had read the first part of *La Recherche* before its publication, he wrote that Ruskin's books were often stupid, fussy, exasperating, wrong, and preposterous, although always significant and always great. These declarations of independence from an author so thoroughly read and analyzed became possible only because Proust had completely absorbed Ruskin. Detaching himself from the old master was a necessary step: Proust believed that one must renounce what one loves in order to re-create it. "The salutary strength of a more forceful personality than his own can enslave an artist, but this servitude is not unlike the beginnings of freedom. He then achieves an exquisite blend of obedience and freedom."*

* Adriana Hunter's translation. *La force bienfaisante d'un tempérament plus puissant que le sien peut asservir un artiste mais cette servitude n'est pas loin d'être le commencement de la liberté. On atteint alors l'exquis, le mélange d'obéissance et de liberté.* "Les Beaux-Arts et l'Etat," in *Contre Sainte-Beuve* (1971), 496.

Noting with glee the huge differences in background and temperament of Proust and Ruskin, Richard Macksey remarks that Proust might well have declared, like his character Swann after years of suffering at the hands of Odette, that the object of his adoration was not his type.[2] Ruskin's puritanical, Scottish-Evangelical background, his moralizing, his ultimate role as prophet of social and ethical renovation, all contrast markedly with Proust's half-Catholic–half-Jewish heritage, his indifference to doctrinal concerns, his ease in a secular society. Ruskin traveled relentlessly, Proust retired early to his cork-lined room. And indeed, since Ruskin is mentioned so rarely in *La Recherche*, one could reasonably ask what Proust gained from the years he had spent poring over Ruskin. The truth is that the debt to Ruskin is considerable, as proved by Proust's correspondence, the evolution of his style, and the ultimate construction of his novel, but the lessons he carried away from the old master were so thoroughly absorbed that they are not easy to detect.

Proust used both ends of the telescope in his reading and appreciation of Ruskin. Using the distance lens, he made out the principles that would underlie the architecture of his own oeuvre; using the close-up lens, he focused on Ruskin's exquisitely minute descriptions, which he emulated in his own depictions of flowers and clothes. Proust had learned that "the greatest thing a human soul ever does in this world is to see something, and to tell what it saw in a plain way . . . To see clearly is poetry, prophecy, and religion—all in one."[3]

By the time Proust had abandoned his work on *Jean Santeuil*, he had written a thousand pages, consisting of loosely related fragments (autobiographical material, descriptions of nature, literary criticism, sketches of characters that were intended to appear in the novel). At best they were chapters of a book: he knew that the unifying structure necessary to shape them into a novel was lacking. Ruskin showed him the way. As Proust explained in a note to his translation of *Sesame and Lilies*, "Ruskin arranges side by side, mingles, maneuvers, and makes shine together all the main ideas—or images—which appeared with some disorder in the course of his lecture. . . . But in reality the fancy that leads him follows his profound affinities which in spite of himself impose on him a superior logic. So that in the end he happens to have obeyed a kind of secret plan which, unveiled at the end, imposes retrospectively on the whole a sort of order and makes it appear magnificently arranged up to this final apotheosis."[4] The revelation that the scaffolding needed for the construction of his novel could rise from his deep and hidden self allowed Proust to move forward.

He left behind *Jean Santeuil*. Instead, three years after the publication of his second Ruskin translation, he started *La Recherche* confident that he would be able to give form to his novel. Nothing was more important to him than the construction of the novel and nothing was more impossible for early readers to detect. True, the last pages of *Time Regained* echo the first pages of *Swann's Way* and illuminate all the themes sounded there as though in an overture, but that does not become evident until the reader has made his way through the intermediate volumes, a difficulty compounded by the fact that the first readers of *Swann's Way*, which appeared in 1913, did not experience this epiphany until the publication of *Time Regained* in 1927, fourteen years later.

Proust knew that French readers were likely to have at most a sketchy notion of Ruskin's work. For that reason alone, Proust could not use Ruskin to flesh out and announce one of his characters, which is what he does when he evokes Saint-Simon in regard to Charlus, the aristocratic grandee so imbued with the prerogatives of true nobility, or quotes Mme de Sévigné, who symbolizes maternal love and is thus naturally linked to the Narrator's mother and grandmother. There is one amusing instance of Proust's overt use of Ruskin: "Sesame" is the password for those seeking admission to Jupien's male brothel, into which the Narrator stumbles and where he finds Charlus chained to an iron bedstead and whipped. But Proust doesn't stop there. He has Jupien, who is surprisingly well read for a former vest maker, joke with the Narrator about the regrettable lack of lilies in his establishment and, for good measure, explain that he had seen the French translation of Ruskin's *Sesame and Lilies* in Charlus's drawing room.

However, an alert reader acquainted with Ruskin's work will find his shadow hovering over *La Recherche*. The book about a church the Narrator reads before falling asleep in the first page of *Swann's Way* may well be an allusion to *The Bible of Amiens*, and *Time Regained* concludes with the Narrator tripping over paving stones in the courtyard of the hotel of the Prince de Guermantes. The sensation revives for the Narrator the memory of walking on the uneven mosaic paving in St. Mark's Basilica, like the one in the Murano Basilica described by Ruskin that "waved like the sea."

Indeed, Proust's first visit to Venice in 1900, which provided indispensable material for the Narrator's and his mother's crucial visit to La Serenissima in *The Fugitive*, can be seen as a pilgrimage to a Ruskin shrine. Proust traveled with his mother, Reynaldo Hahn, and Marie Nordlinger, the Englishwoman who had helped him with the translation. The young people spent hours in St. Mark's reading from Ruskin's *Stones of Venice*, and climbed up ladders to inspect closely the details of capitals they had previously studied in Ruskin's drawings. The significance of capitals would have eluded them without Ruskin's guidance. At San Giorgio degli Schiavoni, they examined Carpaccio paintings that Ruskin claimed to have discovered. The use Proust made of these works leaves *Stones of Venice* far behind, but Proust acknowledged that Ruskin had opened his mind to their beauty. "[Ruskin] will allow my mind to enter where it previously had no access for he is the gateway."[5] Later, Proust once again recalled his debt to Ruskin, *the discoverer, exalter, and devotee** of Carpaccio, and for his admiration of the *divine* Venetian, who was to figure prominently in *La Recherche*, inspiring the wonderful Fortuny gowns worn by Albertine: "these Fortuny gowns, faithfully antique but markedly original, brought before the eye like a stage decor, and with an even greater evocative power since the decor was left to the imagination, that Venice saturated with oriental splendour where

---

* My translation. *Le découvreur, le chantre, le dévôt.* Marcel Proust to Auguste Marguillier, in Proust, *Lettres*, 385.

they would have been worn and of which they constituted, even more than a relic in the shrine of St. Mark, evocative as they were of the sunlight and the surrounding turbans, the fragmented, mysterious and complementary colour. Everything of those days had perished, but everything was being reborn, evoked and linked together by the splendour and the swarming life of the city, in the piecemeal reappearance of the still-surviving fabrics worn by the Doges' ladies."* After Albertine's death the Narrator goes to Venice—the visit echoes Proust's own visit with his mother, Reynaldo, and Marie—and looks at the Carpaccios, reading them subjectively as Ruskin always did. Standing before the painting of the *Patriache di Grado*, he recognizes the coat Fortuny had made for his friend. For a moment he is filled with melancholy. "A while ago, this dress evoked Venice for me and gave me the desire to leave Albertine; now the Carpaccio where I see it evokes Albertine and makes my stay in Venice painful."[6]

Carpaccio is also used in a very different context. Like Ruskin, who had drawn attention to the way Carpaccio's Venice evoked the Orient, Proust suggests that Paris is transformed during the war into an exotic capital crowded by colorful military men.

---

* 3:837. *ces robes de Fortuny, fidèlement antiques mais puissamment originales, faisaient apparaître comme un décor, avec une plus grande force d'évocation même qu'un décor, puisque le décor restait à imaginer, la Venise tout encombrée d'Orient où elles auraient été portées, dont elles étaient, mieux qu'une relique dans la châsse de Saint-Marc évocatrice du soleil et des turbans environnants, la couleur fragmentée, mystérieuse et complémentaire. Tout avait péri de ce temps, mais tout renaissait, évoqué pour les relier entre elles par la splendeur du paysage et le grouillement de la vie, par le surgissement parcellaire et survivant des étoffes des dogaresses. 3:295.*

As in 1815 there was a march past of allied troops in the most [disparate] uniforms; and among them, the Africans in their red divided skirts, the Indians in their white turbans were enough to transform for me this Paris through which I was walking into a whole imaginary exotic city, an oriental scene which was at once meticulously accurate with respect to the costumes and the colours of the faces and arbitrarily fanciful when it came to the background, just as out of the town in which he lived Carpaccio made a Jerusalem or a Constantinople by assembling in its streets a crowd whose marvelous motley was not more rich in colour than that of the crowd around me. Walking close behind two zouaves who seemed hardly to be aware of him, I noticed a tall, stout man in a soft felt hat and a long heavy overcoat, to whose purplish face I hesitated whether I should give the name of an actor or a painter, both equally notorious for innumerable sodomist scandals.*

The sudden apparition of Baron de Charlus on the prowl for a young soldier may also have been inspired by the

* 4:332–33. *Comme en 1815 c'était le défilé le plus disparate des uniformes des troupes alliées; et parmi elles des Africains en jupe-culotte rouge, des Hindous enturbannés de blanc suffisaient pour que de ce Paris où je me promenais, je fisse toute une imaginaire cité exotique, dans un Orient à la fois minutieusement exact en ce qui concernait les costumes et la couleur des visages, arbitrairement chimérique en ce qui concernait le décor, comme de la ville où il vivait Carpaccio fit une Jérusalem ou une Constantinople en y assemblant une foule dont la merveilleuse bigarrure n'était pas plus colorée que celle-ci. Marchant derrière deux zouaves qui ne semblaient guère se préoccuper de lui, j'aperçus un homme gras et gros, en feutre mou, en longue houppelande et sur la figure mauve duquel j'hésitai si je devais mettre le nom d'un acteur ou d'un peintre également connus pour d'innombrables scandales sodomistes. 3:623.*

effeminate men portrayed in Carpaccio's paintings. As Ruskin had pointed out, they all had pretty legs and delightful costumes.

Giotto is another artist with a place of honor in the novel whom Proust discovered under the guidance of Ruskin. During their trip to Venice, Marcel Proust and Reynaldo Hahn went to Padua to see the Giotto frescoes representing the Virtues and Vices in the chapel of the Madonna dell'Arena. Proust puts them to use to a comical effect when he endows his great creation, Charles Swann, with Ruskin's artistic tastes.

The reader first meets Swann as a friend of the Narrator's family, at their country house in Combray at a time when the Narrator is still a child. It is Swann who gives him reproductions of Ruskin's favorite painters, Bellini, Giotto, Carpaccio, and Gozzoli, and notices the resemblance between the family's kitchen maid and Giotto's Charity:

> the kitchen-maid . . . was a poor sickly creature, some way "gone" in pregnancy when we arrived at Combray for Easter . . . she was beginning to find difficulty in bearing before her the mysterious basket, fuller and larger every day, whose splendid outline could be detected beneath the folds of her ample smock. This last recalled the cloaks in which Giotto shrouds some of his allegorical figures, of which M. Swann had given me photographs. He it was who pointed out the resemblance, and when he inquired after the kitchen-maid he would say: "Well, how goes it with Giotto's Charity?" And indeed the poor girl, whose pregnancy had swelled

and [fattened] every part of her, even including her face and her squarish, elongated cheeks, did distinctly suggest those virgins, so sturdy and mannish as to seem matrons rather, in whom the Virtues are personified in the Arena Chapel.*

Other passersby on the streets of Combray are occasions for tweaking the symbolic meaning of Virtues. Giotto's Justice, for instance, "whose greyish and meanly regular features were identical with those which characterised the faces of certain pious, desiccated ladies of Combray whom I used to see at Mass and many of whom had long been enrolled in the reserve forces of Injustice."†

But the most secret and meaningful allusion to Ruskin appears early in *Swann's Way*. Proust uses Ruskin's description of Benozzo Gozzoli's figure of Abraham to portray the father on the evening when the anguished boy, unable to fall asleep, stays up to wait for his mother. Hearing her mount the

---

* 1:79. *La fille de cuisine . . . était une pauvre créature maladive, dans un état de grossesse déjà assez avancé quand nous arrivâmes à Pâques, et . . . elle commençait à porter difficilement devant elle la mystérieuse corbeille, chaque jour plus remplie, dont on devinait sous ses amples sarraux la forme magnifique. Ceux-ci rappelaient les houppelandes qui revêtent certaines des figures symboliques de Giotto dont M. Swann m'avait donné des photographies. C'est lui-même qui nous l'avait fait remarquer et quand il nous demandait des nouvelles de la fille de cuisine, il nous disait: «Comment va la Charité de Giotto?» D'ailleurs elle-même, la pauvre fille, engraissée par sa grossesse, jusqu'à la figure, jusqu'aux joues qui tombaient droites et carrées, ressemblait en effet assez à ces vierges, fortes et hommasses, matrones plutôt, dans lesquelles les vertus sont personnifiées à l'Arena. 1:84–85.*

† 1:80. *une Justice, dont le visage grisâtre et mesquinement régulier était celui-là même qui, à Combray, caractérisait certaines jolies bourgeoises pieuses et sèches que je voyais à la messe et dont plusieurs étaient enrôlées d'avance dans les milices de réserve de l'Injustice. 1:85.*

stairs, he intercepts and detains her, although he fears his father's reaction. He sees the father as "a tall figure in his white nightshirt, crowned with the pink and violet cashmere scarf which he used to wrap around his head since he had begun to suffer from neuralgia, standing like Abraham in the engraving after Benozzo Gozzoli which M. Swann had given me, telling Sarah that she must tear herself away from Isaac."[*] In the book, the Narrator's father merely wants to calm the boy's near-hysterical anxiety and need for his mother. The intention is benevolent. The curious thing about this crucial passage is that no such engraving done after Gozzoli exists. Proust certainly knew and was inspired by Ruskin's drawing that represents Abraham contemplating the destroyed city of Sodom. This remarkable alteration is thought-provoking. Did Proust, in his refusal to conflate his own life with that of the Narrator, prefer not to allude to the subject of homosexuality in a father-son scene, and choose paradoxically to depict the father as ready to sacrifice his son even though he is giving in to the boy's demand? We will have an explanation a few pages later, when the Narrator wastes no time pointing out that the father's subversion of the order established by his mother and grandmother would have pernicious consequences, namely by allowing him to give in to his nervous condition. One should also not forget that it is during that fateful night that the mother reads aloud for the boy the curiously perverse tale of *François le Champi,* thus reinforcing

* 1:37–38. *Je restai sans oser faire un mouvement; il était encore devant nous, grand, dans sa robe de nuit blanche sous le cachemire de l'Inde dans la gravure d'après Benozzo Gozzoli que m'avait donnée M. Swann, disant à Sarah qu'elle a à se départir du côté d'Isaac. 1:51.*

the link between mother and son and excluding the father. A link that is not purely soothing: "I ought to have been happy: I was not. It struck me that my mother had just made a first concession which must have been painful to her, that it was a first abdication on her part from the ideal she had formed for me, and that for the first time she who was so brave had to confess herself beaten. It struck me that if I had just won a victory it was over her. . . . I felt that I had with an impious and secret finger traced a first wrinkle upon her soul and brought out a first white hair on her head."* Ruskin may be unacknowledged, but his role in opening Proust's eyes to the beauty of certain works of art that would become essential in his novel is undeniable. Other non-French writers, while exciting Proust's curiosity and enthusiasm, did not leave such a profound mark on *La Recherche*.

Proust's correspondence contains ample evidence of his boundless admiration for Robert Louis Stevenson, George Eliot, and Thomas Hardy. Their influence on *La Recherche* is more difficult to spot than Ruskin's, but the qualities he singled out for praise are ones that permeate it. Thus he noted that Stevenson's adventure novels rivaled the best introspective novels: "It is within ourselves that we discover the things that seem exterior to us."[7] His enthusiasm for Eliot and Hardy was even greater. "Hardy did a thousand

---

* 1:39. *J'aurais dû être heureux: je ne l'étais pas. Il me semblait que ma mère venait de me faire une première concession qui devait lui être douloureuse, que c'était une première abdication de sa part devant l'idéal qu'elle avait conçu pour moi et que pour la première fois, elle, si courageuse, s'avouait vaincue. Il me semblait que si je venais de remporter une victoire c'était contre elle [. . .] que je venais de tracer dans son âme une première ride et d'y faire apparaitre un premier cheveu blanc. 1:52.*

times better what I am trying to do," he wrote, marveling at the "admirable geometrical parallelism" he created, the use of repetition and superposition and the way the perception of a character changes so swiftly.[8] George Eliot's *The Mill on the Floss* made a huge impression on him. He scribbled a cryptic mention in one of his notebooks that reads "First page of *The Mill on the Floss*."[9] He probably alludes to the instance of involuntary memory described by the English novelist at the very beginning of the novel, when the unnamed narrator falls asleep; her arms pressing into the arms of the chair provoke a sensation that is transformed into a dream. In it, she is taken many years back to a day when, her arms pressed against the stone wall of a bridge, she observed a little girl playing with her dog. The little girl turns out to be Maggie, the heroine of the story. It is a dream that, as in *La Recherche*, provides the impetus for the narrative. Proust admired Eliot's determination "to exhibit nothing as it should be. I only try," she wrote, "to exhibit some things as they have been or are, seen through such a medium as my own nature has given me."[10] And Proust, who for so many years lacked confidence in his ability, was fascinated by the character of Edward Casaubon, the complex and ultimately maleficent clergyman in *Middlemarch*. Proust revealed part of the reason in *Jean Santeuil*, where he was less reluctant to reveal sources and influences: "We never really know whether we have missed our true vocation. Especially in matters of work we are all of us to a certain extent like Mr. Casaubon in *Middlemarch* who devoted the whole of his life to labours which produced results that were merely trivial and absurd."[11]

The great Russian novelists interested him as much as the English ones. He placed Tolstoy—"a serene god"—very high in the pantheon of artists, far above Balzac, probably because he considered a novel like *Anna Karenina* to be "not the work of an observing eye but of a thinking mind. Every so-called stroke of observation is simply the clothing, the proof, the instance of a law, a law of reason or of unreason, which the novelist has laid bare."* This conception was very close to his own ideal. Proust considered that the mere observation of reality could never result in a work of art. As he put it in a letter to Robert de Montesquiou, whom some consider to have inspired the character of Charlus: "I haven't made one single portrait in my book (except for some monocles), because I am too lazy to write just another version of reality."† The artist had to be able to express general laws, and, in his opinion, Tolstoy did it in a masterful way. This reflection on Tolstoy appears in his notebooks. Proust did not give him any space in *La Recherche*. Dostoyevsky, who in his opinion surpassed all other writers, is the subject of extensive comments and analysis in the course of the novel.

A journalist, Jean de Pierrefeu, asked Proust to name the most beautiful novel he ever read. "It is a difficult question," answered Proust, "I would perhaps give my preference to

* Proust, *By Way of Sainte-Beuve*, 284. *Une œuvre [qui] n'est pas d'observation, mais de construction intellectuelle. Chaque trait dit d'observation, est simplement le revêtement, la preuve, l'exemple d'une loi dégagée par le romancier, loi rationnelle ou irrationnelle. Contre Sainte Beuve* (1971), 658.

† My translation. *Je n'ai fait dans mon livre aucun portrait (sauf pour quelques monocles), parce que je suis trop paresseux pour écrire s'il ne s'agit que de faire double emploi avec la réalité.* Chantal, *Marcel Proust*, 286.

The Idiot." But when Jacques Rivière, Proust's editor and
the head of the *Nouvelle Revue Française,* an influential
literary magazine, asked the writer to commemorate the
centenary of Dostoyevsky in 1921, he refused, claiming his
lack of expertise; he did not know Russian, he had to read
him in awful translations and thus could not judge his style.
"I admire the great Russian with a passion, but I do not
know him well."* Actually, Proust's knowledge of *The Idiot,
Crime and Punishment,* and *The Brothers Karamazov* was
remarkable, as was his familiarity with the works of Tolstoy,
but in 1921 he did not want to tear himself away from his
own work in order to write an article.

The treatment of Dostoyevsky in *La Recherche* is unique.
Straightforward and brilliant literary analysis of his work
is provided in the literature courses the Narrator inflicts
on Albertine. But he also draws unexpected comparisons
between Dostoyevsky and his fictional painter, Elstir. At the
very end of the novel, during a conversation with Gilberte
on the difficulty of recapturing the events of a military cam-
paign, he suggests that the best way would be to proceed
"as Elstir painted the sea, by reversing the real and the
apparent, starting from illusions and beliefs which one then
slowly brings into line with the truth, which is the manner
in which Dostoievsky tells the story of a life."† Dostoyevsky
never reveals the true personalities of his characters at the

* My translation. *J'admire passionnément le grand Russe mais le connais
imparfaitement.* Marcel Proust to Gaston Gallimard, September 27, 1921, in
Proust, *Correspondance Générale* (Paris: Gallimard, 1976), 20:479.

† 4:554. *encore faudrait-il peindre [la guerre] comme Elstir peignait la mer,
par l'autre sens, et partir des illusions, des croyances qu'on rectifie peu à peu,
comme Dostoïevski raconterait une vie.* 3:792.

outset. Neither does Proust, and in a curious letter to Gaston Gallimard he asserts that *The Guermantes Way* has a lot more of Dostoyevsky in its composition (and adds that he hopes Gallimard will excuse the arrogance of the comparison) than the other volumes because the characters will do the contrary of what one expects them to do. There is, however, one constant in their behavior, and that is a passion for reading. Positions, opinions, and sexual orientations may change, but everyone keeps reading in *La Recherche*.

III

" Good readers and bad readers."

A life without books was inconceivable for Proust. Not surprisingly, he made literary taste and reading habits a means of defining his characters. Everybody in *La Recherche* reads: servants and masters, children, parents and grandparents, artists and physicians, even generals. Conversations at dinner tables and among friends are mostly literary. The more sophisticated characters find it natural to speak in quotations; quoting from memory is much appreciated in the Narrator's family. His grandmother, grandfather, and mother excel at this pastime. Proust's own family was addicted to this literary game and he recalled that as his own mother lay dying, she quoted a passage by Molière and a sentence by the playwright Labiche. At the very end, barely able to speak, she mumbled, in a desperate effort to cheer up her son, who was fighting back his tears: "*Si vous n'êtes Romain, soyez digne de l'être.*"[1]

All readers are different and no two readers read the same way. Some readers are good and some are bad. Proust establishes a hierarchy for them in *La Recherche*. Readers are ranked according to their attitudes toward books, and he catalogues with delight those he finds wanting. They vastly outnumber good readers, thus proving the truth of his dictum "People don't know how to read anymore."[2] And every bad reader exemplifies a distinct moral or intellectual shortcoming.

Reading should mean understanding. Unfortunately, that is not always the case. For instance, the family's butler doesn't understand or doesn't want to understand what he reads in the newspaper. During the war, he is the principal source of information, or rather disinformation, for the rest of the staff: every day, "Françoise [the old cook] insisted on the bulletins, of which she understood nothing, being read to her by the butler who understood hardly more of them than she."* Much to the surprise of the Narrator, the man does not seem to grasp that the claim that the invasion has been repulsed cannot be true if the enemy gets closer every day. "But we read the newspapers as we love, blindfold. We do not try to understand the facts. We listen to the soothing words of the editor as we listen to the words of our mistress. We are 'beaten and happy' because we believe that we are not beaten but victorious."†

* 4:319–20. *Françoise se faisait lire les communiqués auxquels elle ne comprenait rien, par le maître d'hôtel qui n'y comprenait pas davantage. 3:612.*

† 4:320. *Mais on lit les journaux comme on aime, un bandeau sur les yeux. On ne cherche pas à comprendre les faits. On écoute les douces paroles du rédacteur comme on écoute les paroles de sa maîtresse. On est battu et content parce qu'on ne se croit pas battu mais vainqueur. 3:612.*

When military strategy is not involved, Françoise, for her part, understands what she reads, but fails to make the necessary connection between what she has just learned and real life, thus revealing a form of heartlessness: "The tears that flowed from her in torrents when she read in a newspaper of the misfortunes of persons unknown to her were quickly stemmed once she had been able to form a more precise mental picture of the victims."[*] One evening, at the mythic grandparents' house in the village of Combray, the kitchen maid suffers appalling pains. She has very recently given birth. The Narrator's mother, who had been warned of the possibility of such a crisis by the doctor who delivered the child, hears her groans, awakens Françoise, and sends her to the grandparents' library with the order to bring the medical dictionary, in which she hopes to find advice. Time passes and Françoise hasn't returned. Frustrated, the mother sends the Narrator for the book. In the library he finds Françoise reading the dictionary and being so moved by the description of afterbirth cramps that she is sobbing violently. The Narrator succeeds in convincing her to put down the dictionary and go help the poor maid. But once in the kitchen and faced with the reality of pain, Françoise wipes her tears and offers neither help nor consolation: ". . . at the sight of those very sufferings the printed account of which had moved her to tears, she relapsed into ill-tempered mutterings."[†]

---

[*] 1:120. *Les torrents de larmes qu'elle versait lisant le journal sur les infortunes des inconnus se tarissaient vite si elle pouvait se représenter la personne qui en était l'objet de façon un peu précise. 1:117.*

[†] 1:121. *et à la vue des mêmes souffrances dont la description l'avait fait pleurer, elle n'eut plus que des ronchonnements de mauvaise humeur. 1:117.*

Her colleague, the young footman, intent on proving to his relatives back at the farm that he had become a sophisticated Parisian, steals the Narrator's books and copies from them quotations with which he peppers haphazardly the letters he writes home. The surreal absurdity of these learned sayings' lack of relevance doesn't bother him; he is unconscious of it. For Françoise as for the footman, books are foreign objects and they see no relation between what they describe and their own lives.

Proust is even harsher on the same subject with the university professor Brichot. Like Françoise, Brichot never connects his reading to his inner life, and therefore fails to grasp the universal beauty and truth of certain texts. His being a professor of literature makes the posturing, petty criticism, and lack of insight particularly shocking. For instance, Brichot is unable to make allowances for Balzac's hasty composition and unpolished style, or to understand the power he exercises over his readers. In the case of Chateaubriand, one suspects that Brichot's mind is closed to him for the bizarre reason that Chateaubriand's aristocratic origins annoy him. Baron de Charlus, who has the nature of a true artist, uncharacteristically refuses to argue with Brichot over the genius of the author of *Mémoires d'outre-tombe*. He senses that the effort would be wasted on a pedant obsessed with etymology and grammar, ignorant of life, and willing to sacrifice the true affection he had for a modest laundress in order to please the despotic Mme Verdurin, who feels insulted by the lowly and in her eyes shameful connection. Her soirees are the only social pleasure he knows. How could he capture the beauty and complexity of a great book? The professor of literature is immune to any literary passion. In general, Proust has little regard for academics. As he put it, the professor drones on about Cicero while the budding artist reads Rimbaud or Goethe. "I was no less struck," reflects the Narrator, "by the thought that what were perhaps the most extraordinary masterpieces of our day had emerged not from the Concours Général . . . but from the frequentation of paddocks and fashionable bars."* In 1887, Proust as a high school student represented his lycée at this very competition, the Concours Général, but failed to win any prize.[3]

Conscientious and predictable students do not fare much better than their professors. Robert de Saint-Loup, the Narrator's best friend, a prize-winning pupil in school, a brilliant army officer whose discussions of military strategy fascinate the Narrator, and a nephew of the Duke de Guermantes, is well read and likes to discuss books. But does he grasp what literature is all about? I don't think so, and neither does the Narrator. Saint-Loup's feelings for books are artificial. They do not stem from his inner self. His tastes vary with his politics, or the whims of fashion. For example, at the turn of the nineteenth century a young man in the swing of things had to be romantic and admire Victor Hugo. Naturally, Saint-Loup conformed. His obtuseness is made apparent when, for no better reason than his conviction that romantics stand higher, he undertakes to make fun of his

---

* 4:179. *Je ne fus pas moins frappé de penser que les chefs-d'œuvre peut-être les plus extraordinaires de notre époque sont sortis non du concours général, d'une éducation modèle, académique, à la Broglie, mais de la fréquentation des «pesages» et des grands bars. 3:488.*

uncle, Baron de Charlus, behind his back, because for the older man, Racine, whom he worships, is a much greater writer than Hugo. The absurdity of making exclusionary choices in literature does not enter Saint-Loup's mind, and he even allows the vagaries of his love life to alter his literary taste. "But in reality," the Narrator remarks, "Robert's love of Letters was in no sense profound, did not spring from his true nature, was only a by-product of his love of Rachel [his mistress], and had faded with the latter at the same time as his loathing for voluptuaries and his religious respect for the virtue of women."*

Saint-Loup is handsome, charming, well-born, and rich. Rachel, the first love of his life, is a third-rate actress when their affair begins and, unbeknownst to him, started out in life as a prostitute. However, she is so clever, and so sure of her artistic sense and her taste in literature—which is actually genuine and interesting according to the Narrator—that Saint-Loup is completely under her spell, all the more so because she refuses to be bought by money, jewels, or plain kindness. In a desperate effort to win her over, Saint-Loup tries to convince her of his intellectual leanings. Of course he fails: reading is not an instrument of seduction. It is something you do for yourself in complete solitude.

Another man incapable of understanding that one has to read for oneself and not in order to play a role in society is

---

* 3:91. *En réalité l'amour de Saint-Loup pour les Lettres n'avait rien de profond, n'émanait pas de sa vraie nature, il n'était qu'un dérivé de son amour pour Rachel, et il s'était effacé avec celui-ci, en même temps que son horreur des gens de plaisir et que son respect religieux pour la vertu des femmes. 2:573.*

the Narrator's school friend, Bloch. The Narrator is a little younger, and Bloch exerts a degree of intellectual influence over him. It is for example Bloch from whom the Narrator first learns about the great contemporary writer Bergotte, a personage who is to play an important role in *La Recherche*. But Bloch's affectations are excessive. Eager to shock, determined to distance himself from the "bourgeois," happily unaware of his own total lack of elegance, he sees himself as an aesthetic dandy. His search for originality leads this ostensibly intelligent man to utter the most absurd pronouncements in the most grating manner. True to form, the first time he appears on the scene he ridicules the Narrator's admiration for Musset, coming across as a brutal buffoon: "Hearing me confess my admiration for the *Nuit d'Octobre*, he had burst out in a loud bray of laughter like a bugle-call, and said to me: 'You really must conquer your vile taste for A. de Musset, Esquire. He is a bad egg, one of the very worst, a pretty detestable specimen. I am bound to admit, natheless, that he, and even the man Racine, did, each of them, once in his life, compose a line which is not only fairly rhythmical but has also what is in my eyes the supreme merit of meaning absolutely nothing. One is *"La blanche Oloossone et la blanche Camyre,"* and the other *"La fille de Minos et de Pasiphaë."'"*

---

* 1:88. *En m'entendant lui avouer mon admiration pour la Nuit d'Octobre, il avait fait éclater un rire bruyant comme une trompette et m'avait dit: «Défie-toi de ta dilection assez basse pour le sieur de Musset. C'est un coco des plus malfaisants et une assez sinistre brute. Je dois confesser, d'ailleurs, que lui et même le nommé Racine, ont fait chacun dans leur vie un vers assez bien rythmé, et qui a pour lui, ce qui est selon moi le mérite suprême, de ne signifier absolument rien. C'est: «La blanche Oloossone et la blanche Camire» et «La fille de Minos et de Pasiphaë». 1:92.*

This absurd remark of Bloch's (actually borrowed by Proust from Théophile Gautier) and the aggressive vulgarity of his expressions brand him from the outset. He never improves. In fact, he can get worse, as shown by his condescending remark about *Stones of Venice*: "[Bloch having asked me] why I had come to Balbec (although it seemed to him perfectly natural that he himself should be there) and whether it had been 'in the hope of making grand friends,' and I having explained to him that this visit was a fulfillment of one of my earliest longings, though one not so deep as my longing to see Venice, he had replied: 'Yes, of course, to sip iced drinks with the pretty ladies, while pretending to read the *Stones of Venighce* by Lord John Ruskin, a dreary bore, in fact one of the most tedious old prosers you could find.'"* Like Charlus confronted by Brichot's abysmal lack of taste, the Narrator does not bother to argue with Bloch, but his old school friend tumbles from his pedestal, because to be unable to appreciate Racine or Ruskin is the sign of a barbarian.

Literature is also discussed among the young Balbec girls. During his first trip to Balbec, a seaside resort in Normandy, modeled on Cabourg, the Narrator makes friends with a group of young girls, first spotted on the beach. Athletic, passionate about bicycling and swimming,

* 2:96. *Bloch m'ayant demandé pourquoi j'étais venu à Balbec (il lui semblait au contraire tout naturel que lui-même y fût) et si c'était «dans l'espoir de faire de belles connaissances», comme je lui avais dit que ce voyage répondait à un de mes plus anciens désirs, moins profond pourtant que celui d'aller à Venise, il avait répondu: «Oui, naturellement, pour boire des sorbets avec les belles madames, tout en faisant semblant de lire les Stones of Venaïce, de Lord John Ruskin, sombre raseur et l'un des plus barbifiants bonshommes qui soient.» 1:608.*

and somewhat childish in their tastes for society games, they nonetheless discuss literature, although not at a very sophisticated level. They are still students at a lycée and worried about exams, they cram rather than read. During an outing with the Narrator they argue about an essay, the subject of which is an improbable conversation between Sophocles and Racine, and they all agree that in order to impress the professor, they have to quote well-known critics rather than express personal views. The Narrator takes an ironical view of this exercise, but he does notice that greater knowledge of literature confers on one of them, Andrée, an undisputable authority over the rest of the gang.

Similar literary authority is going to be wielded by Oriane, Duchess de Guermantes, the toast of Parisian high society. She is fond of using books to shock her circle of friends and impress them with her intellectual superiority, but she does so with talent and humor. Émile Zola's novels and politics were at the time considered scandalous, so that when she declares Zola to be a poet at dinner in the presence of the old, conservative, and narrow-minded Princess of Parma, she puts the old lady into a state of intense trepidation, much to the amusement of the mischievous Duchess and some of her guests:

"But Zola is not a realist, Ma'am, he's a poet!" said Mme de Guermantes, drawing inspiration from the critical essays she had read in recent years and adapting them to her own personal genius. Agreeably buffeted hitherto, in the course of the bath of wit, a bath stirred up specially for her, which she was taking this evening and which, she considered, must be particularly good for her health, letting herself be borne up by the waves of paradox which curled and broke one after another, at this, even more enormous than the rest, the Princesse de Parme jumped for fear of being knocked over. And it was with a catch in her voice, as though she had lost her breath, that she now gasped: "Zola a poet!"

"Why, yes," answered the Duchess with a laugh, entranced by this display of suffocation. "Your Highness must have remarked how he magnifies everything he touches. You will tell me that he only touches . . . what brings luck! But he makes it into something colossal. His is the epic dungheap! He is the Homer of the sewers!"*

Of course Oriane knows what she is doing. Her guests are her orchestra, and as the conductor she knows when to have them play fortissimo and when to restore calm. Thus we see her allude to Darwin while evoking the curious reproduction strategy of flowers, a display of learning that

* 2:766. «Mais Zola n'est pas un réaliste, madame! c'est un poète!» dit Mme de Guermantes, s'inspirant des études critiques qu'elle avait lues dans ces dernières années et les adaptant à son génie personnel. Agréablement bousculée jusqu'ici, au cours du bain d'esprit, un bain agité pour elle, qu'elle prenait ce soir, et qu'elle jugeait devoir lui être particulièrement salutaire, se laissant porter par les paradoxes qui déferlaient l'un après l'autre, devant celui-ci, plus énorme que les autres, la princesse de Parme sauta par peur d'être renversée. Et ce fut d'une voix entrecoupée, comme si elle perdait sa respiration, qu'elle dit: —Zola un poète!
—Mais oui, répondit en riant la duchesse, ravie par cet effet de suffocation. Que Votre Altesse remarque comme il grandit tout ce qu'il touche. Vous me direz qu'il ne touche justement qu'à ce qui . . . porte bonheur! Mais il en fait quelque chose d'immense; il a le fumier épique! C'est l'Homère de la vidange! 2:406.

leaves her dinner guests, who have never read *The Origin of Species*, speechless. And she draws on her excellent memory to quote a Victor Hugo poem, both to renew her husband's admiration for her wit, intelligence, and culture, and to make fun of his ignorant mistress, who is incapable of such prowess. For the Duchess, reading is less a source of enjoyment than a wonderfully subtle social instrument of domination.

Her husband, the Duke, is polished enough to know that one is expected to appreciate literature, but he is ordinarily content to bask in the reflected glory of the Duchess, whose accomplishments, in his opinion, *subjugate* the most erudite guests. Left to his own devices, he stumbles. In a sketch of his character that appears in Proust's posthumously published collection of essays, *Contre Sainte-Beuve*, we see the Duke make a show of retiring to his library in order to read Balzac, so as to avoid his wife's guests. The only problem is that all the books on his shelves have the same blond calf's leather bindings, and instead of one of Balzac's novels, he takes down the volume of a third-rate novelist and never realizes his mistake.

Another bad reader is Mme de Brissac, a guest at the Guermantes, who condemns Victor Hugo because he is interested in social hardship and forces monstrosities on his readers: "A distressing spectacle from which we should turn away in real life, that's what attracts Victor Hugo."* She likes books to take her away from life's ugliness and judges them by their subject. Her silliness is equal to that of the

* 2:764. *Un spectacle pénible dont nous nous détournerions dans la vie, voilà ce qui attire Victor Hugo. 2:405.*

Duke de Guermantes, who refuses to buy a wonderful still life by Proust's emblematic painter Elstir because it represents a bunch of asparagus. Why would I pay three hundred francs for a bunch of asparagus? he asks by way of explanation, taking great pride in the originality of his remark.

The Duchess de Guermantes's aunt, Mme de Villeparisis, is a lady of learning and a talented painter, whose father presided over a celebrated political and literary salon where as a girl she knew all the famous writers and artists of the day. When we meet her she is busy writing her memoirs. In the eyes of Proust, she commits the ultimate reader's sin: she judges authors who were her contemporaries by the figure they cut in society. For instance, Alfred de Vigny, incidentally ranking together with Baudelaire as one of Proust's favorite poets, bored her to death.[4] Besides, he didn't know how to hold his hat! Her nephews' admiration for Balzac irritates her: he was a man dressed in ridiculous clothes and undertook to describe an aristocratic society in which he was never received. Mme de Villeparisis's opinions about writers are a spoof of the theories of the great literary critic Sainte-Beuve, who held that knowing an author's character, morals, religion, and comportment was indispensable for assessing the value of his work. This theory was so abhorrent to Proust that he wrote *Contre Sainte-Beuve*, arguing passionately that it represented the negation of all that a true writer is about. According to Proust, an artist does not express his inner self—the self that is never exposed in everyday life and is the only self that matters—in conversation, or even in letters. To look at the artist's life in order to judge the work is absurd. And Proust, as if to prove his point, will create in Vinteuil a composer of genius who while he lived never seemed to be more than a modest piano teacher in the village of Combray, hardly respected by his acquaintances. Swann, so deeply moved by the beauty of his music, cannot imagine that it was written by his country neighbor, whom he considered *une vieille bête*—an old fool.

A few of Proust's characters are passionate readers. They constitute what Proust calls *une franc-maçonnerie des lettrés*, a secret society that allows immediate and otherwise unaccountable complicity. Such is the taste for Saint-Simon that binds Swann, the elegant Parisian, to the Narrator's no-nonsense, provincial grandfather, or the shared enjoyment of Balzac's novels that is one of the links between Swann and Charlus, or, still more surprisingly, the attraction that draws the Narrator's modest and pure grandmother to Charlus, whom in other avatars we see as a violent, insolent, homosexual grandee. A conversation about Mme de Sévigné enables her to detect under the Baron's abrasiveness an unexpected sensitivity.

It is a complicity that brings about a species of telegraphic communications among readers, one that is regularly practiced in the Narrator's family. The grandfather is not an anti-Semite, but all the same he pays close attention to the origins of his grandson's friends, a subtle reminder that this part of the action takes place in the 1890s, a time when the Dreyfus affair was raging in France.[5] The Narrator's family is Catholic, and the grandfather is probably convinced of Dreyfus's culpability, which would explain his interest in the boy's schoolmates. Proust himself was a staunch and active Dreyfusard, like his Jewish mother and his brother, but for many years his father and some of his friends were not. So he knew that honorable people could disagree on this subject. Clearly, the grandfather is not fanatical and has not allowed the affair to alter his friendship with Swann or to lead him to refuse to receive young Bloch, but the Jewish question is on his mind and he does pride himself in being able to detect Jews among them even if their names are not immediate giveaways. After a few innocuous questions, he makes up his mind and puts his family on guard by quoting a seemingly innocent line:

> [Then,] to show us that he had no longer any doubts, [he] would merely look at us, humming under his breath the air of:
>
> > *What! do you hither guide the feet*
> > *Of this timid Israelite*
>
> or of
>
> > *Sweet vale of Hebron, dear paternal fields,*
>
> or, perhaps, of
>
> > *Yes, I am of the chosen race.*[*]

One imagines the giggles of the assembled family, but the final inside joke is that the first quote and the third one,

* 1:90. *Pour nous montrer qu'il n'avait plus aucun doute, il se contentait de nous regarder en fredonnant imperceptiblement: De ce timide Israélite Quoi! Vous guidez ici les pas! ou: Champs paternels, Hébron, douce vallée ou encore: Oui, je suis de la race élue. 1:93.*

so evocative of Racine's style and diction, are Proust's inventions, and the second one was plucked by him out of an obscure eighteenth-century opera by Étienne Méhul. At another time, the Narrator's kind but silly sisters-in-law prove particularly exasperating during a conversation between the grandfather and Swann on the fine points of etiquette followed at the Spanish court commented on by Saint-Simon. How can you admire all this rubbish? one of them exclaims. "Isn't one man as good as the next? What difference can it make whether he's a duke or a groom so long as he's intelligent and kind? He had a fine way of bringing up his children, your Saint-Simon, if he didn't teach them to shake hands with all decent folk. Really and truly, it's abominable."* The elderly gentleman, utterly depressed by the literal turn of mind of his sisters-in-law, convinced that there is no way he can continue to chat with Swann about subjects that delight them, turns to his daughter. "Just tell me again that line of yours which always comforts me so much on these occasions. Oh, yes: 'What virtues, Lord, Thou makest us abhor!' How good that is!"†

This reading mainly for amusement does not entail the great effort of introspection required by a real reader,

---

* 1:28. *Est-ce qu'un homme n'est pas autant qu'un autre? Qu'est-ce que cela peut faire qu'il soit duc ou cocher, s'il a de l'intelligence et du cœur? Il avait une belle manière d'élever ses enfants, votre Saint-Simon, s'il ne leur disait pas de donner la main à tous les honnêtes gens. Mais c'est abominable, tout simplement. 1:43.*

† 1:28. *Rappelle-moi donc le vers que tu m'as appris et qui me soulage tant dans ces moments-là. Ah! oui: «Seigneur, que de vertus vous nous faites haïr!» Ah! comme c'est bien! 1:43.* The line is from Corneille, *Pompée.*

for whom a good book does not offer a conclusion he accepts but constitutes an incitement to think for himself. But certain characters become so obsessed with literature that fiction becomes inseparable from reality. Such a reader is Baron de Charlus, one of Proust's most complex creations.

A homosexual reader: Baron de Charlus

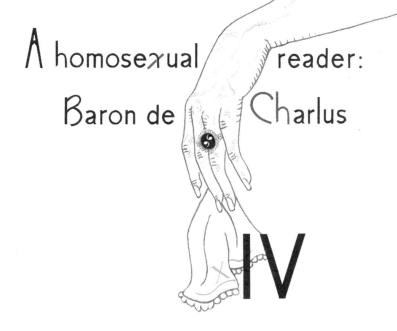

IV

Baron Palamède de Charlus is one of the strongest, most complicated characters of *La Recherche*. Tragic and wildly entertaining, he is the younger brother of the Duke de Guermantes, and thus a member of the noblest and most ancient family of the Proustian realm. The Guermantes seem to live as if the French Revolution had never happened and would feel at home at the court of Louis XIV. One consequence of their inbred rejection of the bourgeois republic is that they consider the President of the Republic a nonperson. In fact, their close friend, Swann, a Jewish roturier and a fashionable Parisian at ease both inside and outside the aristocratic world of Faubourg Saint-Germain, takes a quasi-aesthetic delight in submitting to their prejudices, and never dares confess in their presence that he accepts invitations from the President to the Elysée Palace. The Guermantes owe their allegiance to the Pretender, Count de Chambord, exiled in Austria. They visit him there every year to pay their respects.

Charlus owes his surname to a personage mentioned by Saint-Simon, and his very unusual first name either to a minor character in *Capitaine Fracasse* who distinguished himself during the First Crusade, or to a minor Greek god alluded to in a poem that appears in Balzac's novel *The Peasants*. His more striking traits also have a literary origin. They were inspired by Vautrin, Balzac's great creation. Charlus stands out in *La Recherche* not only as the character with the most literary and aristocratic pedigree but also as one of its most passionate readers, the great connoisseur of Saint-Simon, Balzac, Mme de Sévigné, and Racine. But he is no ordinary reader: his tortured psyche finds in books its nourishment, justification, and solace for his sexual inversion.

Rank, titles, alliances, and past glory are Charlus's obsessions; his knowledge of genealogies and ancient privileges unbeatable, and he exults in his unshakable conviction that he stands at the apex of French society. His prickliness about deference due to rank is legendary in the Faubourg Saint-Germain, and forms an important facet of his personality. The other side of the coin is his homosexuality, which he tries hard to conceal; it explains many of the contradictions of his personality. But Charlus is much more than a caricature of an overweeningly proud aristocrat or a closeted homosexual consumed by his tastes. His musical taste is impeccable and he is a surprisingly good pianist. If he had had sufficient self-discipline, he might have been a good or perhaps even a very good writer. Homosexuality accounts for a great deal of his complexity. As the Narrator explains, "the tiny dislocation of a purely physical taste, the slight blemish in one of the senses [explains] why the world of poets and musicians, so firmly barred against the Duc de Guermantes, opens its portals to M. de Charlus."*

Three writers, Saint-Simon, Mme de Sévigné, and Balzac, are of paramount importance to Charlus, providing him with a frame of reference and coloring his conversation. Saint-Simon is an obvious fit with the Baron de Charlus. Though few people would think that the position of dukes in the ancien régime was threatened, Saint-Simon was convinced of it, and catalogued with furor and passion all encroachments on their prerogatives at court. Any innovation in court etiquette, any advantage given to foreign princes or royal bastards, was met with rage. The ignorance of the King in those matters ignited his more violent sarcasms, and he observed the functioning—what he called the *mechanics* of the court with a relentless eye and reported on it with savage irony. As the Baron sees it, the world in which rank and prerogatives are sacrosanct is also crumbling. Saint-Simon's jeremiads therefore seem timely and prophetic. But one needs stamina as well as enthusiasm to know the *Memoirs* well; they run to forty volumes. It is therefore not surprising that few of Proust's characters have really read them. In addition to Charlus, only Swann, the Narrator, and his grandfather quote from them with ease in

* 3:682. *Un petit déplacement de goût purement physique, . . . la tare légère d'un sens, . . . expliquent que l'univers des poètes et des musiciens, si fermé au duc de Guermantes, s'entr'ouvre pour M. de Charlus. 3:170.*

order to rejoice in Saint-Simon's astonishing style and the unsurpassed portraits of his contemporaries.

There is a special reason for the Narrator's interest in the Duke's memoirs: his hunch that the rules that governed conduct at the court of Louis XIV could apply with equal force in a very different context, that of the sleepy little town of Combray. Proust used Saint-Simon to prove that they did. I should add that he worked tirelessly at this sort of connection, one of the themes of *La Recherche* being that identical rules of conduct may, like laws of nature, govern very different persons and circumstances. Thus he found an analogy between the schedule of Aunt Léonie (the invalid who never ventured outdoors) and the immutable routine of Louis XIV's day, as well as her power over her servant Françoise and that of the King over his subjects, and he showed that social rank in the provinces was no less fixed or less well understood than at the court in Versailles. No overstepping of boundaries was ever allowed: "People at Combray might have kind hearts and sensitive natures, might have adopted the noblest theories of human equality, yet my mother, when a footman showed signs of forgetting his place, began to say 'you' and gradually slipped out of the habit of addressing me in the third person, was moved by these presumptions to the same wrath that breaks out in Saint-Simon's *Memoirs* whenever a nobleman who is not entitled to it seizes a pretext for assuming officially the style of 'Highness,' or for not paying dukes the deference he owes to them and is gradually beginning to [dispense with it]."*

* 3:397–98. *Les gens de Combray avaient beau avoir du cœur, de la sensibilité, acquérir les plus belles théories sur l'égalité humaine, ma mère, quand*

Charlus, who knows the text as well as Swann and the Narrator, of course appreciates it differently. Seeing himself through the prism of the *Memoirs*, he attempts to live them. At home, Charlus likes to impersonate Louis XIV as Saint-Simon described him, following the etiquette the King had invented for Versailles, so that, for instance, instead of treating his guests with the politeness normal for a man of his milieu in fin de siècle France, he would enact for his own pleasure a sort of tableau vivant of the court: "I was not aware, moreover, that at home, in the country, at the Château de Charlus, he was in the habit after dinner (so much did he love to play the king) of sprawling in an armchair in the smoking-room, letting his guests remain standing round him. He would ask for a light from one, offer a cigar to another and then, after a few minutes' interval, would say: 'But Argencourt, why don't you sit down? Take a chair, my dear fellow,' and so forth, having made a point of keeping them standing simply to remind them that it was from him that they must receive permission to be seated."*

---

un valet de chambre s'émancipait, disait une fois «vous» et glissait insensiblement à ne plus me parler à la troisième personne, avait de ces usurpations le même mécontentement qui éclate dans les Mémoires de Saint-Simon chaque fois qu'un seigneur qui n'y a pas droit saisit un prétexte de prendre la qualité d'«Altesse» dans un acte authentique, ou de ne pas rendre aux ducs ce qu'il leur devait et ce dont peu à peu il se dispense. 2:821.

* 2:817. *J'ignorais, du reste, que chez lui, à la campagne, au château de Charlus, il avait l'habitude après dîner, tant il aimait à jouer au roi, de s'étaler dans un fauteuil au fumoir, en laissant ses invités debout autour de lui. Il demandait à l'un du feu, offrait à l'autre un cigare, puis au bout de quelques instants disait: «Mais, Argencourt, asseyez-vous donc, prenez une chaise, mon cher, etc.», ayant tenu à prolonger leur station debout, seulement pour leur montrer que c'était de lui que leur venait la permission de s'asseoir. 2:448.*

This attitude did not necessarily endear him to his guests. But when he played the same royal role for the benefit of his servants, it was received with great enthusiasm. They sensed that they had been promoted to the status of courtiers: "I was reminded of the things I had heard about M. de Charlus's servants and their devotion to their master. One could not quite say of him as of the Prince de Conti that he sought to give pleasure as much to the valet as to the minister, but he had shown such skill in making of the least thing that he asked of them a sort of personal favour that at night, when his [servants] were assembled round him at a respectful distance, and after running his eye over them he said: 'Coignet, the candlestick!' or 'Ducret, the nightshirt!' it was with an envious murmur that the rest used to withdraw, jealous of him who had been singled out by his master's favour."*

All this playacting and Charlus's astonishing touchiness about rank are on display in one of the great comic scenes in *La Recherche.* Charlus crushes M. and Mme Verdurin, the bourgeois art lovers who do not seat him in the place of honor, offering it instead to a provincial marquis. In their naïveté, they had supposed that a marquis always trumps a baron. The gaffe gives M. de Charlus the opening to deliver

* 2:816. *Je me rappelai ce que j'avais entendu raconter des domestiques de M. de Charlus et de leur dévouement à leur maître. On ne pouvait pas tout à fait dire de lui comme du prince de Conti qu'il cherchait à plaire aussi bien au valet qu'au ministre, mais il avait si bien su faire des moindres choses qu'il demandait une espèce de faveur, que, le soir, quand, ses valets assemblés autour de lui à distance respectueuse, après les avoir parcourus du regard, il disait: «Coignet, le bougeoir!» ou: «Ducret, la chemise!», c'est en ronchonnant d'envie que les autres se retiraient, envieux de celui qui venait d'être distingué par le maître. 2:447.*

a lecture on his family's extraction and alliances. He ends by rattling off all his titles, exactly like Saint-Simon when he thinks he has been slighted by a breach of etiquette, and, with consummate impertinence, he concludes when M. Verdurin apologizes: "Why, that's not of the slightest importance, *here*! . . . I could see at a glance that you were out of your depth."*

And at the end of the book, when the glorious Charlus, heir or cousin of so many great noblemen and ruling princes, has been brought low by humiliations and illness, and is attended only by his old lover, Jupien, the vest maker, his degradation is compared by Proust to that of the great homosexuals of the seventeenth century, the Duke de La Rochefoucauld, the Prince d'Harcourt, and the Duke de Berry, who according to Saint-Simon spent all their evenings gambling with their valets and associated with no one who could be named. However, even in the final moments of disgrace, neither they nor Charlus forgot the gestures of politeness, such as the art of doffing one's hat, so essential to the life of Versailles that even the King did not dispense with them. So we see Charlus on the Champs-Elysées, where Jupien has brought him to take the air, greet Mme de Saint-Euverte, once the butt to his endless and scurrilous sarcasms, with a grand and courtly movement.

Except in that scene from the very end of Charlus's life, Saint-Simon is used to caricature the Baron's peculiarities. The role of Mme de Sévigné, in contrast, is to demonstrate his sensitivity. We have seen earlier that a common

* 3:318–19. *Cela n'a aucune importance, ici . . . J'ai tout de suite vu que vous n'aviez pas l'habitude. 2:758.*

admiration for Mme de Sévigné's letters had brought about an improbable understanding between him and the Narrator's grandmother, when they met in Balbec at Mme de Villeparisis's rooms. The grandmother had immersed herself in the author in whom, as Proust would say, she reads herself. Her love for her own daughter made her able to recognize as genuine all of Mme de Sévigné's emotions. The grandmother's attitude was that of absolute empathy, and she was so used to the fact that many people considered the affection between the mother and daughter depicted by her favorite author exaggerated that she is *astonished* to find the rather alarming Charlus grasping Sévigné's truth thoroughly and appreciating her feelings. She saw that he had a delicacy, a sensibility that was quite feminine. Little did she know how right she was.

The conversation between the grandmother and Charlus is unintentionally revealing. It takes place at the beginning of the novel, before Charlus's sexual proclivities have been revealed; he does his best to be circumspect and maintain an appearance of virility. But won over by the grandmother's artlessness, he drops his guard and speaking with her about love and Mme de Sévigné, he unconsciously allows his sensitivity and his vulnerability to appear. He suddenly shows himself as he really is. His voice would give him away if the other people in the room were attentive enough to decipher it. "M. de Charlus not only revealed a refinement of feeling such as few men ever show; his voice itself, like certain contralto voices in which the middle register has not been sufficiently cultivated, so that when they sing it sounds like an alternating duet between a young man and a woman, mounted, when he expressed these delicate sentiments, to its higher notes, took on an unexpected sweetness and seemed to embody choirs of bethrothed maidens, of sisters, pouring out their fond feelings."* He then allows himself a very feminine gesture: "At that moment, noticing that the embroidered handkerchief which he had in his pocket was exhibiting its coloured border, he thrust it sharply down out of sight with the scandalised air of a prudish but far from innocent lady concealing attractions which, by an excess of scrupulosity, she regards as indecent."† And when Mme de Villeparisis, who has been listening to the conversation, declares the extreme love of the mother for the daughter unnatural, she provokes Charlus to say: "what matters in life is not whom or what one loves . . . it is the fact of loving . . . The hard and fast lines with which we circumscribe love arise solely from our complete ignorance of life,"‡ telling words for a man of his nature.

Important as Saint-Simon and Mme de Sévigné are to Charlus, the Narrator, and his family, Balzac's role both in the novel in general and in the conception of Charlus is much more pervasive and unexpected, if only because

* 2:118. *M. de Charlus ne laissait pas seulement paraître une finesse de senti-ment que montrent en effet rarement les hommes; sa voix elle-même, pareille à certaines voix de contralto en qui on n'a pas assez cultivé le médium et dont le chant semble le duo alterné d'un jeune homme et d'une femme, se posait au moment où il exprimait ces pensées si délicates, sur des notes hautes, prenait une douceur imprévue et semblait contenir des chœurs de fiancées, de sœurs, qui répandaient leur tendresse 1:626.*

† 2:119. *avec la mine effarouchée d'une femme pudibonde mais point innocente dissimulant des appas que, par un excès de scrupule, elle juge indécents. 1:627.*

‡ 2:118. *L'important dans la vie n'est pas ce que l'on aime, c'est d'aimer . . . Les démarcations trop étroites que nous traçons autour de l'amour viennent seulement de notre grande ignorance de la vie. 1:626.*

Proust never claimed to be particularly fond of the great nineteenth-century novelist. Indeed, if one were to name Proust's favorite authors, Balzac would not necessarily be at the top of the list. One would first think of Racine, Saint-Simon, George Eliot, Thomas Hardy, or Baudelaire, all writers he admired with unqualified enthusiasm. Proust's attitude toward Balzac is different; he found so much to reprove in his work that their very real affinities are often obscured. He wrote at length about Balzac in *Contre Sainte-Beuve*, a collection published posthumously containing criticism, some of which takes the form of conversations with his mother, as well as sketches that he later used, in a more developed form, in *La Recherche*. He complained about a certain lack of elegance in Balzac's style and the excessive explanations of his characters' feelings (Proust prefers to evoke). Balzac's obsession with the ways in which money is made, and his interest in the world of bankers and lawyers and shopkeepers, are completely foreign to Proust, who never bothers to say anything concrete about the fortune of the Verdurins, beyond the assertion that they are colossally wealthy, or, for that matter, about that of the Narrator. Of course, he appreciated Balzac's power of invention, as well as the stroke of genius by which characters reappear in successive and otherwise separate novels. But this guarded appreciation is not a sufficient explanation of the constant references to Balzac all through *La Recherche*.

"Readers interpret the great books of the past in the light of their obsessions,"[1] wrote Proust, and that is certainly the way he read Balzac. Proust's notes contain a revealing statement about Balzac: he singles out the novelist's audacious treatment of sexual deviations. As a homosexual, he reveled in Balzac's boldness and the originality of homosexual themes, which showed that "Balzac was acquainted even with those passions which the rest of the world ignores, or studies only to castigate them."* Balzac did in fact write at length about homosexuals and lesbians without ever pronouncing a moral judgment. This neutrality, and the willingness to plunge into the worlds of Sodom and Gomorrah, must have endeared him to Proust, and may explain why he read Balzac so assiduously, and made such striking use of him in *La Recherche*.

Most often when Proust brings a writer into the action of his novel he has one of his characters quote from the work and identify it. This is how he deals with Mme de Sévigné, Saint-Simon, Victor Hugo, and Baudelaire. This is also what usually happens when Proust wants to allude to Balzac. But there are some strange and interesting exceptions. One sometimes stumbles on a sentence or a short passage that has little connection with the surrounding text, and it turns out that there is a link to Balzac, as if unconscious memory had been at work, reminding Proust of a passage and prompting him to incorporate it. Unless, perhaps, he was only amusing himself and testing his reader's attention.

For instance, late in *La Recherche*, in *The Captive*, Mme Verdurin orchestrates the disgrace of M. de Charlus by having his lover, the violinist Charles Morel, brutally reject him after a concert given in her house. She cannot resist the impulse to do it, although the thought that

---

* 3:421–22. *Balzac a connu jusqu'à ces passions que tout le monde ignore, ou n'étudie que pour les flétrir. 2:839.*

the incident might ruin her party does cross her mind. Proust offers a strange and unexpected explanation of her irrational action. "There are certain desires, sometimes confined to the mouth, which, as soon as we have allowed them to grow, insist upon being gratified, whatever the consequences may be; one can no longer resist the temptation to kiss a bare shoulder at which one has been gazing for too long and on which one's lips pounce like a snake upon a bird."*

What can naked shoulders possibly have to do with Mme Verdurin and her concert? If the metaphor seems outlandish, and unconnected to what Mme Verdurin is meditating, there is a reason for it: it comes straight out of Balzac's *Lily in the Valley*. In one of the strangest scenes of that novel, during a ball, a very young man throws himself passionately on an unknown lady whose perfumed white shoulders have had just such an effect on him. There is nothing logical in the evocation of Balzac at this moment of the novel and thus an explanation is difficult to find. Another completely unexpected secret allusion to Balzac comes very early in *Swann's Way*. During a walk the Narrator as a child takes with his parents near Combray, he is struck by the vision of a lady: "A young woman whose pensive face and elegant veils did not suggest a local origin, and who had doubtless come, in the popular phrase, 'to bury herself' there, to taste the bitter sweetness of knowing that her name, and

* 3:780. *Il y a certains désirs, parfois circonscrits à la bouche, qui, une fois qu'on les a laissés grandir, exigent d'être satisfaits, quelles que doivent en être les conséquences; on ne peut plus résister à embrasser une épaule décolletée qu'on regarde depuis trop longtemps et sur laquelle les lèvres tombent comme le serpent sur l'oiseau. 3:249.*

still more the name of him whose heart she had once held but had been unable to keep, were unknown there, stood framed in a window . . . And I watched her, returning from some walk along a path where she knew that he would not appear, drawing from her resigned hands long and uselessly elegant gloves."[*]

The Narrator has just offered a masterful summary of Balzac's novella *The Deserted Woman*, and has not failed to mention the young woman's gloves, which have a special meaning in the tale. As in the previous example, this invocation of Balzac has nothing to do with the story Proust is telling. The lady never reappears and is never mentioned again. The vision only serves to make the text richer for the reader who recognizes its provenance.

Quite as curious is the Narrator's remark about a valet invited to dinner by Charlus. The man is so elegant in his borrowed clothes that tourists take him for a rich American, but the waiters at the restaurant recognize immediately who he is, "as one convict recognizes another."[†] The simile is curious: granted that members of a profession are apt to identify each other, why connect an overdressed valet with a convict? The answer can be found in a scene at the end of *Splendors and Miseries of Courtesans*, in which the escaped convict, Vautrin, appears in the courtyard of the prison,

---

[*] 1:168. *Une jeune femme dont le visage pensif et les voiles élégants n'étaient pas de ce pays et qui sans doute était venue, selon l'expression populaire «s'enterrer» là, goûter le plaisir amer de sentir que son nom, le nom surtout de celui dont elle n'avait pu garder le cœur, y était inconnu . . . Et je la regardais, revenant de quelque promenade sur un chemin où elle savait qu'il ne passerait pas, ôter de ses mains résignées de longs gants d'une grâce inutile. 1:154.*

[†] 3:362. *Comme un forçat reconnaît un autre forçat. 2:791.*

disguised as a priest, and is detected within minutes by the other convicts. Proust clearly had Balzac on his mind.

Indeed, two of Balzac's great themes have a quintessential importance in *La Recherche*. The first is the cruelty of children toward their parents (as in the story of Goriot, who gives his fortune away to his two daughters and dies, destitute and disconsolate, while they are attending a ball). In Proust's novel it is illustrated by the conduct of Swann's daughter, Gilberte, who is so ashamed of his being a Jew that she is willing to take the name of her stepfather and to hint that she is the illegitimate daughter of a prince of the blood; by the demands for money made by her insatiable daughter on an ailing Berma, the legendary actress, that push her to agree to performances that hasten her death; by Mlle Vinteuil, the composer's daughter, whose liaison with a young woman tortures her father; and finally by Saint-Loup's callous treatment of his loving and vulnerable mother. The second theme is that of "unnatural passions," as for instance in Balzac's *Girl with the Golden Eyes*, the story of a woman's tragic obsession with a troubled young girl, Paquita. The nature of such passions is subject to even more thorough study by Balzac in his story of the relations between a series of young men and Vautrin, a homosexual convict who ends his improbable career as the head of the Paris police. Vautrin plays a central role in *Father Goriot* and in the *Lost Illusions* cycle.

Charlus's homosexuality and its role in *La Recherche* caused Proust considerable anxiety. Early in negotiations with his publisher, Gaston Gallimard, as to the terms on which the volumes following *Swann's Way* would appear, he warned Gallimard repeatedly that Charlus was "a character that I believe is rather new, the virile pederast, enamored of virility, detesting effeminate young men."[*] He specified that the old gentleman picks up a concierge and a violinist, and that the whole thing is rather indecent. For a while Proust thought of placing himself under the protection of Balzac by adding to *Sodom and Gomorrah* a long footnote in the form of a quotation from *Father Goriot* on the subject of the third sex, the term adopted by Balzac. He insisted on his concerns out of worry that the reaction of shocked and indignant readers would cause Gallimard to interrupt the publication of his work in midstream. Gallimard was able to reassure him, and the publication proceeded. But that was not the end of Proust's worries. The public appearance of Charlus caused him another kind of problem.

Proust was very conscious of the curiosity, rampant among his friends, about the models for his characters. Who was the elegant and witty Duchess de Guermantes, who was Odette, the courtesan who ends up marrying the fashionable Swann, much to the distress of his friends? Readers speculated about the possible inspiration for Bergotte, the writer whose name was so similar to that of the philosopher Henri Bergson and whose style was so reminiscent of Anatole France. And, of course, who was the "real" Charlus? All fingers pointed at Count Robert de Montesquiou-Fézensac, a blueblood aristocrat and a gifted writer well known for his insolence, touchiness, and flamboyant homosexuality. Clues

---

[*] My translation. *Un caractère que je crois être assez neuf, le pédéraste viril, épris de virilité, détestant les jeunes gens efféminés.* Marcel Proust to Gaston Gallimard, November 1912, in Proust, *Lettres*, 584.

were abundant. Charlus had his violinist, Morel, Montesquiou had his pianist, Léon Delafosse. As if that were not enough, Proust, courting danger, let slip into his description of Charlus's elegance an allusion to Whistler, who was widely known to have painted a magnificent portrait of Montesquiou.[2] And, later on in the novel, he had Charlus doubt that the Narrator had ever heard of Whistler, thus producing at once an instance of Montesquiou-like insolence and another sign pointing in the direction of Whistler's model.

Another clue, or indeed provocation, concerned pears, a fruit of which Montesquiou was a well-known connoisseur. When Charlus wants to show off to Morel his knowledge of food and talent for tormenting social inferiors, he offers him an impromptu course, not on apples or grapes, but on pears, and berates an unfortunate waiter unable to distinguish among the many different splendid species of that fruit. While Proust obviously couldn't resist playing with fire, at least in this case he was afraid to touch the flame. Not only was he apprehensive about Montesquiou's likely reaction; he also anticipated the heated exchange of letters it would occasion, and the resulting loss of time and energy. His solution was to procrastinate. He sent Montesquiou a copy of *Sodom and Gomorrah* only after a long delay, claiming he didn't have a valuable first edition to offer him.

Montesquiou proved to be an intelligent and perceptive reader: "Vautrin is in fashion and your Charlus has something of him."* Relieved, Proust sent him a long letter explaining the futility of looking for "keys that only open

* My translation. *Vautrin est à la mode et votre Charlus en tient.* Robert de Montesquiou to Marcel Proust, April 17, 1921, in Proust, *Lettres*, 999.

for a moment" and he specified that he had thought for a moment of a Baron Doazan while depicting Charlus, "but later, I abandoned the idea and created a much larger Charlus, entirely invented."* He let the allusion to Vautrin go unanswered. Proust's silences are at least as important as his utterances, and I am convinced that Balzac's straightforward portrayal in Vautrin of a mature homosexual gave Proust courage and showed him the way. After all, did he not say over and over again that intellectual life (and by that he meant life in books) was so much richer, so much more diverse than social intercourse? He learned more of life's ironies and complexities from novels than from people. "Real life, life at last laid bare and illuminated—the only life in consequence which can be said to be really lived—is literature."†

Balzac's Vautrin is an escaped convict who reigns over the criminal class because he is in effect its unofficial banker. He is entrusted with the proceeds of burglaries and murders, and distributes funds as he sees fit. He does not like women, declares a policeman intent on capturing him, late in *Father Goriot*. A careful reader would not need the hint, having noticed how Vautrin loses no time in proposing an astonishing arrangement to the handsome student Rastignac, his fellow boarder in a Parisian pension. Rastignac rejects the offer. He has retained a spirit of prudence

---

* My translation. *Mais je l'ai laissé ensuite et j'ai construit un Charlus beaucoup plus vaste et entièrement inventé.* Marcel Proust to Robert de Montesquiou, April 18 or 19, 1921, in Proust, *Lettres*, 1003.

† 4:464. *La vraie vie, la vie enfin découverte et éclaircie, la seule vie par conséquent pleinement vécue, c'est la littérature.* 3:725.

and independence. It is another beautiful youth, Lucien de Rubempré in *Splendors and Miseries of Courtesans*, who will become Vautrin's passion, his creature, and finally his victim.

Charlus and Vautrin live in worlds separated by an incalculable social distance, but they have many things in common. Each is extremely powerful in his milieu. Charlus can make or break a lady's position in society with a single word. Vautrin's influence in the hard labor camp where he served his sentence is compared by Balzac to that of a duke and peer in civil society. Each of them in his own sphere is feared, and rightly so. Masterminding a murder is practically second nature to Vautrin. Charlus, we are told, is capable of killing a man. Morel, who knows him well, is quite convinced that he can be physically dangerous, and admits to the Narrator that he is afraid of him. Both are vigorous and fierce but their most striking feature is a certain magnetic look. Their eyes are like pistols aimed at a target.

Both are given to orating, and both are nonconformists. Vautrin is in open revolt against society; Charlus's insolence and recklessness in pursuit of sexual satisfactions are capable of undermining a social position even as unassailable as his. If they care to be, they are delightful with women. Mme Vauquer, the cagey owner of the pension where Vautrin and Rastignac lodge, plies him with favors; Charlus can charm effortlessly any lady he chooses to favor by his attention, including the Narrator's grandmother. Their attempted and unsuccessful seductions of young men—Rastignac in the case of Vautrin, and the Narrator in that of Charlus—are very similar. Vautrin offers out of the blue to make the fortune of the penniless student (through an outrageous scheme that involves a murder). Although Rastignac refuses, he will remain all his life terrified of Vautrin. Similarly, Charlus dangles before the Narrator, who has never thought of asking for the slightest favor, the possibility of a fantastic ascent in society. As if to tease his reader, Proust has Charlus allude to Balzac at this very moment: "What one cannot do alone in this life, because there are things which one cannot ask, or do, or wish, or learn by oneself, one can do in company, and without needing to be thirteen, as in Balzac's story."[*] He is referring to *Ferragus*, in which thirteen men band together to plan and execute murderous revenges. Not surprisingly, Charlus's violence and exorbitant demands frighten the Narrator; he escapes as shaken as Rastignac. Their successes are also similar. Proust was so impressed by the scene in which, moved by the physical beauty of Lucien de Rubempré, Vautrin picks him up on the side of a road, that he re-created it. Charlus is similarly smitten by the mere sight of Morel on the train station platform in the little Normandy town of Doncières.

Charlus at his most furious also evokes Vautrin. The "snakes of foam and spray," the olive-colored, bilious juice that Charlus seems to spit when the Narrator's obtuseness exasperates him, conjure up Vautrin's awful "streams of saliva" when he is seized by the police. However, the resemblance between the two characters remains superficial. Their inner selves are completely different. One feels that

[*] 2:828. *Ce qu'on ne peut pas faire seul dans la vie, on le peut à plusieurs et sans avoir besoin d'être treize comme dans le roman de Balzac.* 2:457.

Proust took the outer envelope of Vautrin and poured into it a very different man.

Charlus's rages are not the expression of his nature. He works up these furious eruptions in order to terrorize his interlocutors, but deep down he is a sensitive old woman with very literary tastes, which is an aspect of his nature that is recognized not only by the Narrator's grandmother but also by his sister-in-law, Oriane, Duchess de Guermantes, who describes him as having the heart of a woman: *"C'est un cœur de femme, Mémé."* Her use of his nickname Mémé, which means Granny in French, adds to the impression she wants to give and infuriates her husband.

Charlus identifies strongly with certain literary characters. We have seen him play at being Louis XIV, as described by Saint-Simon. He is more serious when he is immersed in Balzac. Discussing books with members of the Verdurins' little clan, he is under the illusion that they aren't aware of his homosexuality, and names, when asked which are his favorite Balzac novels, *Lost Illusions, The Girl with the Golden Eyes, A Passion in the Desert,* and *Sarrazine.* Homosexuality is a principal theme of the first two books; the passion referred to in the third one is that of an officer for a panther; the eponymous principal character of *Sarrazine* is neither a normal man nor a woman but a castrato. As we have seen earlier with the example of Mme de Sévigné, Charlus's literary choices reveal passions he wishes to conceal. And it becomes obvious, when he speaks of certain novels, that he experiences deeply the emotions associated with them. In *Lost Illusions,* there are times when he feels fleetingly close to Vautrin, for instance when Vautrin stops the coach in which he is traveling so as to take a nostalgic walk around Rastignac's château. Charlus maintains that this is the most beautiful scene in the whole book. But he feels even greater affinity to a woman, the heroine of the novella *The Secrets of the Princesse de Cadignan*.

As a young woman, the Princess was well known for her numerous love affairs, and had ruined more than one admirer. By the time she reaches thirty—middle age for Balzac's women—she retires from Parisian society, having lost her fortune but retained her beauty. She falls in love with Daniel d'Arthez, a writer who is a paragon of virtue, and lives in fear that he will be told of her past indiscretions. This is a concern with which Charlus identifies completely. Unlike Vautrin, he does not carry his homosexuality lightly, and does not realize that it is common knowledge. For instance, he gets upset when his brother, Basin, the Duke de Guermantes, in whom he has never confided, makes in his presence a feeble and innocent joke about his special tastes. Guilt, foreign to Vautrin, is very much an element of Charlus's personality. "'*The Secrets of the Princesse de Cadignan!*' he exclaimed, 'what a masterpiece! How profound, how heart-rending the evil reputation of Diane, who is afraid that the man she loves may hear of it. What an eternal truth, and more universal than it might appear!'" Charlus at the time is afraid that the family of his lover Morel might learn about his homosexuality and intervene to protect the young man against him. Now that "he had suddenly begun to identify his own situation with that described by Balzac, he took refuge, as it were, in the story, and for the calamity which was perhaps in store for him and which he certainly feared, he had the consolation of finding in his own anxiety what Swann and also Saint-Loup would have called something 'very Balzacian.'"*

Proust uses another aspect of this novella to show the woman hidden in Charlus. Diane, the heroine of the story, takes intense care in the selection of her dresses. Charlus has their design so precisely in mind that he compliments Albertine, the young girl with whom the Narrator is in love, on her costume not only by comparing it with that of Diane but also by going into the most intricate details of design and color. "M. de Charlus was almost the only person capable of appreciating Albertine's clothes at their true value; his eye detected at a glance what constituted their rarity, their worth; he would never have mistaken one material for another, and could always recognise the maker."† He is gentle with Albertine and tolerant of the limitations of her culture. It is as though the identification with Diane kept Vautrin in check, bringing out the best qualities in Charlus, those of a generous and fundamentally good woman.

---

* 3:427. *«Les Secrets de la princesse de Cadignan! s'écria-t-il, quel chef-d'œuvre! comme c'est profond, comme c'est douloureux, cette mauvaise réputation de Diane qui craint tant que l'homme qu'elle aime ne l'apprenne! Quelle vérité éternelle, et plus générale que cela n'en a l'air! comme cela va loin!» . . . Et maintenant que depuis un instant il confondait sa situation avec celle décrite par Balzac, il se réfugiait en quelque sorte dans la nouvelle, et à l'infortune qui le menaçait peut-être, et ne laissait pas en tout cas de l'effrayer, il avait cette consolation de trouver, dans sa propre anxiété, ce que Swann et aussi Saint-Loup eussent appelé quelque chose de «très balzacien». 2:845.*

† 3:424. *Il n'y avait guère que M. de Charlus pour savoir apprécier à leur véritable valeur les toilettes d'Albertine; tout de suite ses yeux découvraient ce qui en faisait la rareté, le prix; il n'aurait jamais dit le nom d'une étoffe pour une autre et reconnaissait le faiseur. 2:842.*

When Charlus is in his Saint-Simon mode, he is comical, somewhat ridiculous, but when he is in his Balzac mode, I find him moving and sensitive. The homosexual reading of Balzac is close to his heart.

In sharp contrast with Charlus, the Narrator has no literary lineage whatsoever. No character invented by another writer is involved in his creation. The Narrator is a purely Proustian character. Literature plays an important role in his life, however, because he recognizes in himself one of the greatest characters of French literature, Racine's Phèdre.

RACIne;
a
second
language

Of all the writers who nourished Proust none is more present in the development of the novel than Racine. Ever since he was a schoolboy, Proust had a predilection for Racine. It is customary in French literature classes to debate which of the two giants of French seventeenth-century drama, Corneille or Racine, is greater. Proust's essay comparing them has survived, and though he is respectful of Corneille and his heroic view of the world, his preference for Racine, the poet of the *réalité farouche,* is clear. "Being passionate about Racine simply means loving the most profound, tender, painful, and sincere intuition about so many charmed and martyred lives, just as being passionate about Corneille means loving the loftiest realization of a heroic ideal in all its honest beauty and unfailing pride."* The schoolboy strove for balance by giving Corneille his fair share, but the novelist will not even try to conceal his preference. Proust's lack of interest in Corneille is manifest: there are few references to Corneille in *La Recherche,* while Racine is a constant emotionally charged presence, from the Narrator's childhood in Combray to the dénouement of his love affair with Albertine. Moreover, Racine's plays are used by Proust both as a comical example of the homosexual reading of works of literature and as tragic illustrations of the ravages wrought by rejected love and jealousy.

Proust looks closely at three plays by Racine, *Phèdre* and the two biblical plays about Jewish queens, *Esther* and *Athalie.* The biblical plays were written for Saint-Cyr, the girls' school created by Mme de Maintenon, the morganatic wife of Louis XIV. Girls acted in all the roles. In order to give every pupil a chance to perform, Racine increased the

---

* Adriana Hunter's translation. *Aimer passionnément Racine ce sera simplement aimer la plus profonde, la plus tendre, la plus douloureuse, la plus sincère intuition de tant de vies charmantes et martyrisées, comme, aimer passionnément Corneille, ce serait aimer dans toute son intègre beauté, dans sa fierté inaltérable, la plus haute réalisation, d'un idéal héroïque.* Proust, *Juvenilia,* in *Contre Sainte-Beuve* (1971), 332.

size of the casts through the use of choruses, large groups of girls standing around on the stage with nothing much to do. If we remember that Proust was convinced that a passionate reader is always the reader of his own self, always imagining himself in the text he is immersed in, we can easily conceive how Proust, and consequently some of his characters, transformed in their imagination these young beauties into boys. And indeed, whenever the attention of one of Proust's exemplary three old queens in *La Recherche* (the Marquis de Vaugoubert, the fatuous diplomat married to an equine wife; Bloch's rich uncle Nissim Bernard; and, of course, Charlus) chances upon a group of idle young men—bellhops, waiters, or young dandies milling around in a salon—they are irresistibly reminded of Racine's choruses. For instance, Vaugoubert is ecstatic to learn that some of the secretaries of the embassy to which he is to be posted might be of his sexual persuasion. The Narrator, observing his excitement, imagines that the ambassador is recalling the lines of Esther, who has hidden her Jewish origins and those of her companions from her husband, Assuérus, King of Persia, that allude to the young Israelites of her court gathered by Mordecai:

> *Meanwhile his love for our beloved race*
> *Has filled this palace with young Jewesses.*
> *Here he (the excellent ambassador) can care for them*
> *and teach their souls and minds.**

* My translation. *Cependant son amour pour notre nation/A peuplé ce palais des filles de Sion,/Il (l'excellent ambassadeur) met à les former son étude et ses soins. 2:249.*

Naturally, M. de Vaugoubert is afraid of being perceived as a homosexual, giving the Narrator the opportunity for another quotation from Racine. The two lines spoken by Queen Esther, who is just as anxious as Vaugoubert to keep her secret, encapsulate the rule that the diplomat has adopted for his conduct in public:

> *The King unto this day knows not who I am,*
> *And this secret keeps my tongue still enchained.*[*]

The use of Racine in this case, however, goes beyond simple comic effects: it reinforces the analogy between Jews and homosexuals advanced by Proust in his jeremiad on the "accursed race" at the beginning of *Sodom and Gomorrah*, in which he likens sodomites to Jews, "brought into the company of their own kind by the ostracism to which they are subjected, the opprobrium into which they have fallen, having finally been invested, by a persecution similar to that of Israel, with the physical and moral characteristics of a race."[†] Proust does not maintain this dramatic accent when he moves to the Grand Hotel in Balbec, where the Narrator and his grandmother stay. He reverts quickly to irresistible parodies that have the designs Nissim Bernard has on a young waiter as their

---

[*] My translation. *Le Roi jusqu'à ce jour ignore qui je suis,/Et ce secret toujours tient ma langue enchaînée. 2:249.*

[†] 3:17. *rassemblés à leurs pareils par l'ostracisme qui les frappe, l'opprobre où ils sont tombés, ayant fini par prendre, par une persécution semblable à celle d'Israël, les caractères physiques et moraux d'une race. 2:511.*

target. The tone is set by the Narrator, when he compares the Grand Hotel to the Temple of Solomon and the hotel bellhops "to the young Israelites of Racine's choruses," who, except for their day off, lead "the same ecclesiastical existence as the Levites in *Athalie*."* Racine alludes here to the descendants of the Hebrew tribe of Levi assigned to the care of the tabernacle and the temple. Esther and Vaugoubert face the same problem. Both have to hide their identity, so the comparison between them is unexpected but not outlandish. It is more difficult to find common ground between Racine's *Athalie* and the activities of M. Nissim Bernard. The tragedy deals with the lethal clash between Athalie, Queen of Judea, and the Jewish high priest, Joad. Athalie has abandoned the Jewish faith and has massacred all her descendants to make sure that no Jew will ever reign over her kingdom. Unbeknownst to her, a grandson has been saved and is being raised in the Jewish temple. Athalie visits the temple, notices the child, and, although she does not recognize him, demands that he follow her to her palace. He does not let himself be swayed by the Queen and refuses to leave the temple. Eventually, the Jews rebel against Athalie and kill her.

In order to connect the story of the seduction of a young waiter by Nissim Bernard to lines from *Athalie*, Proust has quite a bit of transposing to do. The young waiter takes on the role of Joas, the Jewish child, but instead of resisting the advances of his seducer, the way Joas resists those of

---

* 3:163. *la même existence ecclésiastique que les lévites dans Athalie.* 2:632.

Athalie, he succumbs to them happily. The Racine lines Proust uses work perfectly well but, unlike those he borrowed from *Esther*, have little to do with their original meaning, a distortion that adds considerably to the comic effect.

It is true that the forty years' difference in age between M. Nissim Bernard and the young waiter ought to have preserved the latter from a contact that could scarcely have been agreeable. But, as Racine so wisely observes in those same choruses:

> *Great God, with what uncertain tread*
> *A budding virtue 'mid such perils goes!*
> *What stumbling-blocks do lie before a soul*
> *That seeks Thee and would fain be innocent.*

For all that the young waiter had been brought up "in seclusion from the world" in the Temple-Palace of Balbec, he had not followed the advice of Joad:

> *In riches and in gold put not thy trust.*

He had perhaps justified himself by saying: "The wicked cover the earth." However that might be, and albeit M. Nissim Bernard had not expected so rapid a conquest, on the very first day,

> *Whether in fear, or anxious to caress,*
> *He felt those childish arms about him thrown.*

And by the second day, M. Nissim Bernard having taken the young waiter out,

The dire assault his innocence destroyed.

From that moment the boy's life was altered. He might only carry bread and salt, as his superior bade him, but his whole face sang:

> *From flowers to flowers, from joys to joys*
> *Let our desires now range.*
> *Uncertain is our sum of fleeting years,*
> *Let us then hasten to enjoy this life!*
> *Honours and high office are the prize*
> *Of blind and meek obedience.*
> *For sorry innocence*
> *Who would want to raise his voice?*[*]

Improbably, the majestic and severe *Athalie* is thus found providing a comic accompaniment to the old lecher's

---

[*] 3:225–26. *A vrai dire, les quarante années qui séparaient M. Nissim Bernard du jeune commis auraient dû préserver celui-ci d'un contact peu aimable. Mais, comme le dit Racine avec tant de sagesse dans les mêmes chœurs: Mon Dieu, qu'une vertu naissante,/Parmi tant de périls marche à pas incertains! Qu'une âme qui te cherche et veut être innocente,/Trouve d'obstacle à ses desseins. Le jeune commis avait eu beau être «loin du monde élevé», dans le Temple-Palace de Balbec, il n'avait pas suivi le conseil de Joad: Sur la richesse et l'or ne mets point ton appui. Il s'était peut-être fait une raison en disant: «Les pécheurs couvrent la terre.» Quoi qu'il en fût, et bien que M. Nissim Bernard n'espérât pas un délai aussi court, dès le premier jour, Et soit frayeur encore ou pour le caresser,/De ses bras innocents il se sentit presser. Et dès le deuxième jour, M. Nissim Bernard promenant le commis, «l'abord contagieux altérait son innocence». Dès lors la vie du jeune enfant avait changé. Il avait beau porter le pain et le sel, comme son chef de rang le lui commandait, tout son visage chantait: De fleurs en fleurs, de plaisirs en plaisirs/promenons nos désirs./De nos ans passagers le nombre est incertain/Hâtons-nous aujourd'hui de jouir de la vie!/ . . . L'honneur et les emplois/Sont le prix d'une aveugle et basse obéissance./Pour la triste innocence/Qui voudrait élever la voix! 2:683–84.* Some of the quotes from *Athalie* have been slightly altered by Proust.

seduction of a young man until then unacquainted with the pleasures of the third sex, a quasi-sacrilegious fiddling with the tragedy made possible by Proust's extraordinary familiarity with Racine's texts. This virtual symbiosis between the two writers of genius enabled him to use the seventeenth-century playwright's language as though it were his own, and to apply it to subjects of his choice. Proust confers a similar facility on the Narrator's mother in *La Recherche*, enabling her to quote Mme de Sévigné in preference to confronting her son and expressing her dissatisfaction with his habits in her own words.

Proust's discussion of *Phèdre* in relation to the Narrator shows that this connection goes even further than the adoption of language. *Phèdre* and its eponymous heroine, the Greek princess, have a unique importance in *La Recherche*. The first allusion to the princess occurs in the comparison between her and the Narrator, still a child in Combray, distraught at the thought of parting with his beloved hawthorns: "On the morning of our departure I had had my hair curled, to be ready to face the photographer, had had a new hat carefully set upon my head, and had been buttoned into a velvet jacket; a little later my mother, after searching everywhere for me, found me standing in tears on the steep little path near Tansonville, bidding farewell to my hawthorns, clasping their sharp branches in my arms and, like a princess in a tragedy oppressed by the weight of these vain ornaments, with no gratitude towards the importunate hand which, in curling all those ringlets, had been at pains to arrange my hair upon my forehead."* A great deal is lost in translating this passage, an English-speaking reader being unlikely to recognize immediately the allusion to Phèdre's famous lines *"Quelle importune main en formant tous ces noeuds a pris soin sur mon front d'assembler mes cheveux?"*[1] woven very cleverly into the text, yet another example of Proust's dexterity with a text that had become part of himself.

Phèdre is a leitmotif of the Narrator as he grows up. It is linked to his first love, Gilberte Swann, a childhood friend, with whom he plays regularly in the little park of the Champs-Elysées. His parents don't want to frequent the Swann household, even though M. Swann is an old family friend, because Mme Swann had been a well-known courtesan. The result is that the children see each other only out of doors until the boy manages to be invited to the Swanns alone, finessing the parents' objections. His ruse consists in telling Swann of his admiration for Racine and for the fictional great writer Bergotte, who is a permanent fixture of Mme Swann's salon. Charmed and amused by the boy's precocity, Swann issues the coveted invitation. It is a fact that the Narrator already knows *Phèdre* by heart, and that his reading of Bergotte, whom he has recently

---

* 1:143. *Le matin du départ, comme on m'avait fait friser pour être photographié, coiffer avec précaution un chapeau que je n'avais encore jamais mis et revêtir une douillette de velours, après m'avoir cherché partout, ma mère me trouva en larmes dans le petit raidillon, contigu à Tansonville, en train de dire adieu aux aubépines, entourant de mes bras les branches piquantes, et, comme une princesse de tragédie à qui pèseraient ces vains ornements, ingrat envers l'importune main qui en formant tous ces nœuds avait pris soin sur mon front d'assembler mes cheveux, foulant aux pieds mes papillotes arrachées et mon chapeau neuf. 1:134.*

discovered, has opened his eyes to beauties in *Phèdre* that he had never noticed before. This display of literary taste moves Swann to go further: he proposes not only to introduce him to Bergotte but also to ask the great writer to lend to the boy his little volume on Racine. Bergotte, he adds, is a great friend of my daughter's. The Narrator feels "so keenly how sweet and how impossible it would be for [him] to become [Gilberte's] friend that [he] was filled at once with longing and despair."* He is ready to fall in love, and of course he does.

It is she who will later give the Narrator Bergotte's little volume. From then on, he associates the beauty of these pages with his love for the young girl. Vacations separate them. To console him, his mother offers to let him see Berma, the fictional famous actress of the day and Swann's and Bergotte's great favorite, act in *Phèdre*. He is so excited at the prospect, expects so much pleasure, that not surprisingly he is disappointed by the actual performance. It is only some years later, seeing Berma in *Phèdre* once more, that he realizes how Racine's genius is revealed by the intelligence and subtlety of her art, and comes to understand how difficult it is to appreciate an artist's new interpretation of a familiar masterpiece. "And for this reason it is the really beautiful works that, if we listen to them with sincerity, must disappoint us most keenly, because in the storehouse of our ideas there is none that responds to an individual

* 1:98. *J'éprouvai si vivement la douceur et l'impossibilité de devenir son ami, que je fus rempli à la fois de désir et de désespoir. 1:100.*

impression."* The important law of aesthetics the Narrator has just discovered thus has its source in Racine, and more specifically in *Phèdre*. And once again Proust shows that reading a work of literature as it should be read is really reading about oneself. The final crisis in the relationship between the Narrator and Albertine gives Proust an opportunity to demonstrate the truth of his thesis: we find the Narrator in *The Fugitive* seeing himself as Phèdre.

Having for all practical purposes sequestered Albertine, the Narrator realizes that her presence is a burden, and plans to break with her. But, unexpectedly, it is she who takes the initiative and leaves him without any warning. As the knowledge of her departure sinks in, the Narrator comes to feel that he cannot survive the blow; for the first time he realizes that the lines he has so often read and repeated for himself are the statement of the laws to which he has been subject all his life. This is what *Phèdre* is all about, he says to himself.

Phèdre is consumed by an illicit passion for her stepson Hippolyte. She could accept being separated from him if she was the one who had banished him. But as in the case of the Narrator and Albertine, it is he who decides to leave, with the result that, half demented, Phèdre reveals to him her passion. The young man is unmoved. She grasps the reason: he is in love with another woman. From that moment, she

* 2:339. *Et à cause de cela ce sont les œuvres vraiment belles, si elles sont sincèrement écoutées, qui doivent le plus nous décevoir, parce que, dans la collection de nos idées, il n'y en a aucune qui réponde à une impression individuelle. 2:60.*

pursues him with deadly hatred, although, if he had given any sign of being interested in her, she would have rejected him as an unworthy son and lover. The Narrator explains how the paradox illuminates his own life: "There are things in our hearts to which we do not realise how strongly we are attached. Or else, if we live without them, it is because day after day, from fear of failure, or of being made to suffer, we put off entering into possession of them. This was what had happened to me in the case of Gilberte, when I thought that I was giving her up . . . Or else, if the thing is already in our possession, we feel that it is a burden, that we should be only too glad to be rid of it; and this was what had happened to me in the case of Albertine. But let a sudden departure remove the unwanted person from us, and we can no longer bear to live."* When Albertine proposes to come back, he refuses, convinced that this gesture proves that she indeed loves him. And if she loves him, her presence is unnecessary.

Phèdre is the symbol of *l'amour-maladie*, love experienced as a sickness, which underlies the Narrator's masochistic conception of love. It is foreshadowed and illustrated by the misadventures of Swann and Saint-Loup, which demonstrate that we never love with greater intensity than

---

* 4:40–41. *Il y a dans notre âme des choses auxquelles nous ne savons pas combien nous tenons. Ou bien si nous vivons sans elles, c'est parce que nous remettons de jour en jour, par peur d'échouer ou de souffrir, d'entrer en leur possession. C'est ce qui m'était arrivé pour Gilberte . . . Ou bien si la chose est en notre possession, nous croyons qu'elle nous est à charge, que nous nous en déferions volontiers; c'est ce qui m'était arrivé pour Albertine. Mais que par un départ l'être indifférent nous soit retiré, et nous ne pouvons plus vivre. 3:374.*

when our love is unrequited. That is when jealousy stokes the fire in which we burn. The love-jealousy syndrome is at the root of the Narrator's unhappy but inconsequential love affair with Gilberte. It is explored most fully when the Narrator realizes that he loves Albertine and has lost her. Proust is so straightforward in the surprising identification of his Narrator with Phèdre that one may wonder whether it applies to Proust the man as well as to the Narrator. The reason for indulging this hypothesis is that Phèdre's tragedy has as its cause not only Hippolyte's scorn but also the devastating conviction that her passion for him is immoral and disgraceful. Proust was not a homosexual able to accept or indeed rejoice in his sexual identity. Secrets, shame, and remorse weighed heavily on him. He could never bring himself to reveal his homosexuality to his parents. He must have yearned for "innocent" pleasures with the desperate longing of Phèdre's evocation of the guiltless loves of Hippolyte and her rival Aricie:

> *Alas! full freedom had they*
> *To see each other. Heav'n approved their sighs;*
> *They loved without the consciousness of guilt;*
> *And every morning's sun for them shone clear,*
> *While I, an outcast from the face of Nature,*
> *Shunn'd the bright day, and sought to hide myself.**

* Racine, *Phaedra*, trans. R. B. Boswell. *Hélas! Ils se voyaient avec pleine licence./Le ciel de leurs soupirs approuvait l'innocence;/Ils suivaient sans remords leurs penchants amoureux;/Tous les jours se levaient clairs et sereins pour eux./Et moi, triste rebut de la nature entière/Je me cachais au jour, je fuyais la lumière. Phèdre,* act 4, scene 6.

How could he fail to feel profound empathy with the unfortunate queen guilty of incestuous love, a crime so shameful that she must dread having to confess it to her father Minos who judges in Hades the souls of the dead? "There is more truth in a single tragedy of Racine than in all the dramatic works of Monsieur Victor Hugo,"* declared Baron de Charlus. He was speaking for Marcel Proust.

* 2:118. *Il y a plus de vérité dans une tragédie de Racine que dans tous les drames de monsieur Victor Hugo. 1:626.*

the Goncou*R*ts

VI

Proust's admiration and understanding of Racine—and indeed of Balzac—were very different from his attitude to the Goncourts, two brothers who always wrote together. I would say he took in general a somewhat ironical view of their work. At the end of his life, the irony often turned to sharp criticism. Though there are traces of their *Journal* in *La Recherche*, the Goncourts stood for what Proust considered the nonartist, the mere observer; he found he could delineate his literary goals by juxtaposing their writing with his own.

Jules and Edmond de Goncourt were a quirky pair. Though eight years apart—Edmond, the elder, was born in 1822—after their mother's death in 1848, they spent the rest of Jules's life together. During that entire period, they spent only one day apart. Not only did they live together, they also never signed a book or an article except jointly. They started out as artists, traveling to Algiers and coming back with a stack of drawings and watercolors, but realized quickly that their talent was not up to their ambition. They switched to literature, first as journalists specializing in art criticism and theater reviews, and then to writing history books, biographies, sketches of living authors, and novels. All the while they kept a journal. They became members in good standing of the literary set, and initiated a monthly dinner at a Parisian restaurant, Magny, at which the celebrated novelists of the time, Flaubert, Turgenev, Zola, Maupassant, and Daudet, and historians and philosophers such as Taine and Renan, gathered regularly. When Jules died, Edmond maintained the tradition alone.

Edmond and Jules de Goncourt's novels are hardly read these days in France. Their *Journal* has fared better, but they are best known to the general public for having created the most important of French literary prizes, the Prix Goncourt, which is awarded each year by ten writers who constitute the Académie Goncourt, a literary foundation established by Edmond both to honor his brother and to encourage young and innovative novelists. After Jules died in 1870, Edmond continued the task of describing the literary and social life of the time. He published a first edition of the *Journal* in 1885 that provoked irate protestations from many writers, Zola, Renan, and Taine included. They claimed that quoting out of context shreds of conversations, held at a dinner table or in a restaurant, as the Goncourts had done, was not only an insufferable breach of privacy, it was dishonest. Taken aback, Edmond decided prudently not to publish the text in its entirety during his lifetime. "In a Journal such as the one I'm publishing," he declared, "the absolute truth about the men and women encountered during my life is composed of an agreeable truth—that one likes; but it is almost always tempered by disagreeable truth—that one absolutely doesn't want."* However, parts of their *Journal, a Memoir of Liter-*

* My translation. *Dans un Journal comme celui que je publie, la vérité absolue, sur les hommes et les femmes, rencontrés le long de mon existence, se compose d'une vérité agréable—dont on veut bien; mais presque toujours tempérée par une vérité désagréable—dont on ne veut absolument pas.* Edmond de Goncourt and Jules de Goncourt, *Journal* (Paris: Robert Laffont, 1956), 1:132.

ary Life, were published until 1896, the year Edmond died, and were read with great curiosity. Their malicious gossip was irresistible, as was their mastery of what was known as *l'écriture artiste,* distinguished by the use of rare and archaic words, audacious neologisms, and startling juxtapositions of seemingly conflicting terms. In his will, Edmond gave the Académie Goncourt the responsibility of publishing the entire work twenty years after his death. In fact, the complete edition did not become available to the public until 1956.

The Goncourts occupy an unusual place in *La Recherche.* They are not quoted, though they often serve as a source of anecdotes, and they never serve to illuminate a character's personality. Nor are they the favorite authors of any of Proust's characters. Their *Journal* appears in the most ambiguous form as the subject of a pastiche, several pages long, and is crucial to understanding, first what the Narrator initially perceives as his inevitable failure as a writer, and second his subsequent determination to commence and complete his work. As a result, the Goncourts' importance is more negative than positive. They are used as a foil and never as an ideal.

Proust read the Goncourts quite thoroughly and not only did he absorb their idiosyncratic style but also took advantage of excellent material he could appropriate from their pages. His extraordinary talent for mimicry and his amazing eye for detail allowed him to show off by writing *à leur manière*—in their fashion—whenever he chose to, whether in the pastiche, incorporated in the last volume of *La Recherche,* or to add a finishing touch to the portrait of M. Legrandin, the Combray friend of the Narrator's parents, a parodic figure whose speech is precious, charming, and often obscure. As for the borrowings, I will point out that three of the most comical remarks in the novel come straight from the *Journal*. The first concerns Swann's father. When the old man admits that, although he is crushed by the death of his wife, he only thinks of her for short moments at a time, he is echoing a remark of a famous hostess, Mme Aubernon, a lady of great authority and little charm, whose salon was frequented by Anatole France, who according to the Goncourts confessed that she missed her late mother very much but rarely. The second instance shows how Proust is set off by a remark that amuses him but uses it differently. The Goncourts mention a lady who claims that the telephone is the most amazing invention since *les tables tournantes*. Turning tables, on which Ouija boards were often placed, supposedly allowed the participants to communicate with the other world and were very popular at the time. Proust will have a character go even further in the absurdity. At a concert, "dazzled by the virtuosity of the performers [a countess exclaims], 'It's astonishing! I've never seen anything to beat it.' But a scrupulous regard for accuracy making her correct her first assertion, she added the reservation: 'anything to beat it . . . since the table-turning!'"* The third comical—indeed inane—comment is the assurance proffered by the Princess of Parma's lady-in-waiting: salt spread on the streets is known to stop snowfalls. The Goncourts reported this very same idiocy, uttered by a person in the

* 1:344–45. *Emerveillée par la virtuosité des exécutants, la comtesse s'écria . . . «C'est prodigieux, je n'ai jamais rien vu d'aussi fort.» Mais un scrupule d'exactitude lui faisant corriger cette première assertion, elle ajouta cette réserve: «Rien d'aussi fort . . . depuis les tables tournantes.» 1:294.*

entourage of Princess Mathilde Bonaparte. Once more we see Proust having fun, especially since—as with the incongruous allusions to Balzac—not many readers were able to appreciate fully what he was doing. In other instances, the description of a person excited Proust's imagination. The Princess of Parma's physical appearance and way of dressing, as described by Proust, no doubt reminded readers of Princess Mathilde Bonaparte, the Emperor's cousin, who figures prominently in the *Journal*. Mme Verdurin owes a lot to Mme Aubernon. And Mme de Villeparisis, as a source of anecdotes, may have been inspired by Mme de Beaulaincourt, "in her salon upholstered with yellow silk, full of family portraits, in the middle of which she created a cool atelier of a florist," who also loved to talk about the past. In that case, as Mme de Beaulaincourt was still alive, Proust wrote to a friend that he had changed a detail in order not to make the model too recognizable.[1] The real lady made artificial flowers while the fictional one painted them. But these are details. More important is the difference of judgment on purely literary matters between the two brothers and Proust.

As we have seen, Proust was steeped in the seventeenth century, had not much to say about the literature of the eighteenth century, and was very thoughtful and often enthusiastic about French writers closer to his times, like Balzac, Hugo, and Baudelaire. His taste and support for living artists and the Symbolist poets—Mallarmé, Anna de Noailles, and Henri de Régnier, for instance—was expressed in many articles. The Goncourts, on the other hand, were very dismissive of the great authors of the seventeenth century: "Racine and Corneille have never been anything other than transcribers into French verse of Greek, Latin, and Spanish plays. They have never invented or created anything on their own."[*] Their contemporaries did not fare any better: "I spit on my contemporaries. In the world of letters—and on the highest level—an abasement of judgment, a breakdown of opinions and consciences. The more straightforward, the more choleric . . . ground down by relationships, weakened by compromises, lose in the ambient cowardice the spirit of rebellion, and find it difficult not to consider beautiful everything that succeeds."[†] This judgment had nothing to do with literature: it was a moral condemnation and not a subtle one. For Proust literature had nothing to do with morality.

Subtlety was not the Goncourts' forte. The vulgarity, the crudeness of their criticism was completely alien to Proust, whose shrewd and restrained analysis of style was exemplary. They detested Racine with an irrational violence and bragged that they did not want any work of his in their library. They quoted the most outrageous remarks with glee, making a point of repeating that Théophile Gautier considered that "Racine wrote like a pig,"[‡] and never seemed to consider that quips, coined after many drinks, were not

[*] My translation. *Au fond, Racine et Corneille n'ont jamais été que des arrangeurs en vers de pièces grecques, latines, espagnoles. Par eux-mêmes, ils n'ont rien trouvé, rien inventé, rien créé.* Goncourt and Goncourt, *Journal*, 2:904.

[†] My translation. *Je vomis mes contemporains. C'est dans le monde des lettres, et dans le plus haut, un aplatissement des jugements, un écroulement des opinions et des consciences. Les plus francs, les plus coléreux . . . au frottement des relations, au ramollissement des accommodements, dans l'air ambiant des lâchetés, perdent le sens de la révolte, et ont de la peine à ne pas trouver beau tout ce qui réussit.* Ibid., 2:70.

[‡] My translation. *Racine faisait des vers comme un porc.* Quoted by Annick Bouillaguet, *Proust et les Goncourt* (Paris: Archives des lettres Modernes, 1996), 34.

necessarily fit to print. Their descriptions of society figures of their time were so exaggerated that they seem to be more imaginative than truthful. No one ever accused James de Rothschild of being handsome, but did he really have "a monstrous face, the flattest, basest, and most frightful of batrachian visages, bloodshot eyes, lids like scallops, mouth like a piggy bank and drooling"?* If one were to believe them, Mme Zola's voice when she was upset was as shrill as that of a "foul-mouthed fishwife about to chew you out,"† and Zola had the appearance of a growling dog, ready to bite. But it may well be from the Goncourts that Proust got the idea of introducing a good deal of coarseness in the vocabulary used in the artistic milieu of Mme Verdurin's salon. She herself accuses Brichot of writing like a pig, and is not shocked by Elstir's scatological description of a painting: "Impossible to say whether it was done with glue, with rubies, with soap, with bronze, with sunshine, with crap!"‡ When it came to the essential, the question of what makes a true artist, Proust was very critical of the Goncourts and would probably have been even more cutting if the Prix Goncourt he had received in 1919, and which contributed greatly to his nascent popularity, had not obliged him—if not to have a bust of Edmond de Goncourt in his apartment as he joked—at least "to [take] a good many respectful

---

* My translation. *une monstrueuse figure, la plus plate, la plus basse et la plus épouvantable face batracienne, des yeux éraillés, des paupières en coquille, une bouche en tire-lire et comme baveuse.* Goncourt and Goncourt, *Journal,* 1:923.

† My translation. *Une poissarde prête à vous engueuler.* Ibid., 3:593.

‡ 1:249. *One pourrait pas dire si c'est fait avec de la colle, avec du rubis, avec du savon, avec du bronze, avec du soleil, avec du caca. 1:218.*

precautions when [he had] to talk to him."* To illustrate his reservations, Proust resorted to parody.

The Goncourt pastiche appears toward the end of *Time Regained,* the last volume of the work, in the form of a passage of the *Journal.* As was Proust's custom, he is vague about the date, but the circumstances are the following: At the beginning of the First World War, the Narrator is in the country, staying with his old friend Gilberte, in Tansonville, the house she inherited from her father; it used to be the destination of walks in the countryside around Combray that he and his family used to take when he was a child. Gilberte is now married to Robert de Saint-Loup. A spectacularly courageous cavalry officer he is, serving at the front. Unbeknownst to his wife, he is a homosexual. The Narrator is still obsessed by Albertine—now dead—and, more precisely, by his imperious need to find out whether she had indeed been a lesbian. Since Gilberte had known Albertine ever since they were girls, he grills her about Albertine's tastes in the course of an evening that he and Gilberte spend alone. Finally, it is time to go to bed. The Narrator would have liked to take with him Balzac's lesbian tale, *The Girl with the Golden Eyes,* but Gilberte is reading it, so she lends him instead a recently published volume of the Goncourts' *Journal.* Reading in bed, he chances upon a lengthy passage devoted to the Verdurins and their little clan. The chronology is complicated enough to confuse even a careful reader. Proust's Narrator is most probably reading

* Adriana Hunter's translation. *[Ce qui m'oblige] à beaucoup de respectueuse précaution quand j'ai à parler de lui.* Proust, "Les Goncourt devant leurs cadets," in *Contre Sainte-Beuve* (1971), 642.

in late 1914; the episode described in the pastiche dates from the period covered by *Swann's Way* in the first volume of *La Recherche*, and portrays the Verdurin salon, such as it was, at the time of Swann's affair with Odette, that is to say soon after the Franco–Prussian war of 1870 and perhaps ten years before the Narrator and Gilberte were born. Thus, unlike the Goncourts, the Narrator had not been an eyewitness to all the events concerning the Verdurins' early years; his notion of what they had been like is based on accounts he heard from Swann and perhaps from other elders. One can readily imagine how Proust's Narrator, in his middle age, is immediately attracted to the *Journal* and its reminiscences of people he had met or heard about in his younger days.

The Goncourts—or rather the Goncourts as imagined by Proust in his pastiche—see the Verdurins very differently from the way they were perceived by Swann, or, twenty years later, by the Narrator. In Swann's and the Narrator's version, M. Verdurin is very much the husband whose role is to pay the bills and show his wife in the best possible light; Mme Verdurin is ruthless, gratuitously cruel, and morbidly ambitious. But, as seen by the fictional Goncourts, M. Verdurin is a sensitive artist and Mme Verdurin a charming hostess. This disparity troubles the Narrator, leading him to question his own ability to decipher and describe what he has been told and what he has witnessed. The result is a subtle game of mirrors.

The Narrator has yet to write anything, and is still worried about his possible lack of talent. At the same time, his commentary shows that, for him, literature has nothing to do with the simple description of what one sees. Once more, the Narrator and Proust merge into the same person. Marcel has contempt for the Goncourts' portrayals of people, because he is interested not in what people say, "but the manner in which they said it and the way in which this manner revealed their character or their foibles."* Proust the author expressed exactly the same idea when he wrote to his editor that he was much too lazy to describe what anyone could see. For the Goncourts, the mere outward impression, not the deep personal impression but an impression shared by many, or a superficial conversation, is what leads to literature. For the Proustian Narrator the source of art is quite different: it is not the appearance of an object, of a sunset, that counts: art resides "not in the superficial appearance of his subject but at a depth at which that appearance matters little."† Reality has to be re-created; it is not to be found in descriptions of things observed. Those who refuse to make the introspective effort to understand the origin of an artistic emotion "grow old useless and unsatisfied, like celibates of Art! They suffer, but their sufferings, like the sufferings of virgins and of lazy people, are of a kind that fecundity of work would cure."‡ In his novel, Proust does not mention by name *ces célibataires de l'art* who, quite obviously for anyone in the know, target the unmarried Goncourt brothers; in an article written to celebrate the centenary of Edmond de Goncourt, Proust was more explicit: "This subordination

* 4:287. *mais la manière dont ils le disaient, en tant qu'elle était révélatrice de leur caractère ou de leurs ridicules. 3:587.*

† 4:450. *non dans l'apparence du sujet, mais à une profondeur où cette apparence [importe] peu. 3:715.*

‡ 4:460. *vieillissent inutiles et insatisfaits, comme des célibataires de l'art. Ils ont les chagrins qu'ont les vierges et les paresseux, et que la fécondité dans le travail guérirait. 3:722.*

of every duty regarding society, friends, and family to the duty of serving the truth could have brought M. de Goncourt greatness had he taken the word truth in a wider, deeper sense, had he created more living beings whose descriptions included elements that, unintentionally, brought out something different, extensive, and complementary from the hasty sketches forgotten in his memory. Sadly, instead of this, he observed, made notes and wrote a journal, which is not the work of a great artist, a creator."[*]

Clearly, the Goncourts' conception of literature irritated Proust. He may have tired of Ruskin, he may have criticized Balzac's style, but he never denied how very much their work had enriched his own. In the case of the Goncourts, on the contrary, he does not seem to take them seriously as artists. Yet his fascination with their writing is manifest. The scandalous first publication and the heated discussions it provoked took place when Proust was seventeen. He probably dipped into the *Journal* immediately and was sufficiently amused by the anecdotes and surprised by the style to return to it many times. He read so carefully that he published a Goncourt pastiche in *Le Figaro* in 1908, when he was beginning to write *La Recherche*. The Goncourts may have shown him all the pitfalls, whether the lack of

---

[*] Adriana Hunter's translation. *Cette subordination de tous les devoirs, mondains, affectueux, familiaux, au devoir d'être le serviteur du vrai, aurait pu faire la grandeur de M. de Goncourt s'il avait pris le mot de vrai dans un sens plus profond et plus large, s'il avait créé plus d'êtres vivants dans la description desquels le carnet de croquis oublié dans la mémoire vous apporte sans qu'on le veuille un trait différent, extensif et complémentaire. Malheureusement au lieu de cela, il observait, prenait des notes, rédigeait un journal ce qui n'est pas d'un grand artiste, d'un créateur.* Proust, "Les Goncourts devant leurs cadets," in *Contre Sainte-Beuve* (1971), 642.

introspective effort or the adoption of a complicated, fussy style that a true artist had to avoid, but they also were quite useful in showing how their contemporaries spoke, the idiosyncratic vocabulary of artists and socialites of the second half of the nineteenth century. Proust and the Goncourts were not of the same generation, but when Proust delves into the past of Swann or the Verdurins or any of his Narrator's elders, he re-creates the world of the Goncourts. In consequence being able to borrow many building blocks from them was singularly helpful. When a pretentious provincial lady in the novel uses the word *talentueux*, which was not recognized by the dictionaries of the time, instead of a more usual term, it is because Proust read it in the Goncourts and thought it illustrated perfectly a certain taste for unnecessary complications. The same is true for the word *drôlatique*, used by a relation to describe the Duchess de Guermantes. One of the great achievements of Proust is the singularity of the voice of each of his characters. Since they all speak differently, the reservoir of peculiar expressions found in the *Journal* was precious, and Proust fished in it with great relish.

The Goncourts did not have the profound, personal resonance that Racine, Baudelaire, or Balzac had for Proust, but they stimulated his critical faculty, enriched his knowledge of an era he was too young to have known except secondhand, and in the process helped him find his own voice.

BERGOTTE:
The writer in VII the novel

As we have seen, writers to whom Proust felt close or had read attentively play an essential role in *La Recherche*. So does the fictional writer, Bergotte, who along with Elstir the painter and Vinteuil the musician form the triumvirate of artists at the center of Proust's exploration of aesthetics. Vinteuil and, even more so, Elstir, are subjects of distinct narratives; Bergotte's story is less developed. He first appears not as a person but a name on the spine of a book. On the advice of his friend Bloch, the Narrator starts reading him and soon becomes completely enthralled by his work.

His passion for Bergotte's books is such that they fill him with "a joy that [he] felt [he] was experiencing in a deeper, vaster, more integral part of [himself], from which all obstacles and partitions seemed to have been swept away.""* And the adolescent Narrator acknowledges the miraculous fact that, thanks to Bergotte, he has discovered hidden beauties in everyday objects and texts he thought he knew quite well: "Whenever he spoke of something whose beauty had until then remained hidden from [him], of pine-forests or of hailstorms, of Notre-Dame Cathedral, of Athalie or of Phèdre, by some piece of imagery he would make their beauty explode into [his] consciousness."† The Narrator at this point in the story dreams of becoming a writer but is still very unsure of himself. Are his daydreams of any value? Does he have anything of interest to write about? But he is encouraged by the fact that sometimes he finds in Bergotte an echo of a thought that had taken form in his mind or of an idea he had attempted to describe to his mother or his grandmother. He knows that his father is opposed to his nascent ambition and would like to see him enter the Foreign Service, while the mother and the grandmother support his aspirations. This coincidence of thought between Bergotte and himself boosts his self-confidence to the point that he weeps for joy "upon his printed page as in the arms of a long-lost father"‡ as he

* 1:93. *une joie que je me sentis éprouver en une région plus profonde de moi-même, plus unie, plus vaste, d'où les obstacles et les séparations semblaient avoir été enlevés. 1:95.*

† 1:94. *Chaque fois qu'il parlait de quelque chose dont la beauté m'était restée jusque-là cachée, des forêts de pins, de la grêle, de Notre-Dame de Paris, d'Athalie ou de Phèdre, il faisait dans une image exploser cette beauté jusqu'à moi. 1:96.*

‡ 1:95. *je pleurai sur les pages de l'écrivain comme dans les bras d'un père retrouvé. 1:97.*

realizes that his humble self may have a connection with the godlike artist.

He is so enamored of Bergotte's style, "his form . . . so poetic and so musical,"* his undeniable search for formal beauty, and his intelligence, that he is abashed by the disdainful remarks about him of his father's respected friend, M. de Norpois, the ambassador, during a family dinner. The young man is at a loss for words to defend his idol against the attacks. It is only when he grows older that he realizes that one cannot refute Norpois's arguments because of their complete lack of substance. M. de Norpois is a vacuous and pretentious man, incapable of original thought, a cruel caricature of a career diplomat, afraid of voicing an opinion contrary to the tradition of the French Foreign Service. Not surprisingly, he thinks literature should be a virile production useful to the country. For him art for art's sake (in his mind exemplified by Bergotte) is anathema, and he condemns Bergotte's preciousness. He considers him a mere flute player.

Proving himself a critic as absurd as Sainte-Beuve, who was so detested by Proust, Norpois ends his diatribe against Bergotte by introducing personal details about the writer's life, and unctuously recalls an incident in Vienna where he was posted as ambassador. Bergotte was traveling with a lady who was not his wife and had the presumption to ask to be invited to the embassy. Of course Norpois, in spite of the warm recommendation of the Princess von Metternich,

* 1:533. *sa forme . . . si poétique et musicale. 1:462.*

refused to condone such scandalous behavior, leaving no doubt that it influenced his opinion of Bergotte's work. Without question, in this passage Proust defends his own view of literature, but he also defends one of his early loves, Anatole France, whose style and interests are very similar to the ones attributed to the fictional writer. France himself wrote: "I am sometimes a bit ashamed of my flute playing, although I do have to give myself credit for always trying to give a meaning to my little songs."*

Not much later, Swann invites Marcel to lunch with Bergotte, and the man, no longer just a name, appears on the scene. The young Narrator had a mental image of this writer of genius that he derived from his books. Disregarding Norpois's gossip, he had imagined him as a frail and disappointed old man who had lost his children and had never found consolation. Instead, he has the shock of meeting "a youngish, uncouth, thickset and myopic little man, with a red nose curled like a snail-shell and a goatee beard."†

The contrast illustrates the divergence, which Proust always insisted upon, between the artist in society and the artist at work. According to him, the artist reveals himself only in his creations; his conversation and correspondence are external, incapable of giving access to the inner self, which is all that matters. The Narrator is disappointed during this first encounter not only because Bergotte's physical

* My translation. *A certaines heures, j'éprouve quelque honte à jouer de la flûte, encore que je puisse me rendre ce témoignage que je me suis efforcé de donner un sens à mes petites chansons.* Jean Levaillant, "Notes sur le personnage de Bergotte," *Revue des sciences humaines*, January–March 1952, 43.

† 1:530. *un homme jeune, rude, petit, râblé et myope, à nez rouge en forme de coquille de colimaçon et à barbiche noire. 1:460.*

appearance does not match his expectations but also because his conversation is hardly fascinating. He wrote so well and yet his speech was affected, emphatic, and monotonous. This trait was inspired by Anatole France, the author of many delectably ironic novels, who was known to be something of a bore in society. Like many Proustian characters, Bergotte (whose name is close enough to "Bergson" for the typo in the first edition replacing "Bergotte" with "Bergson" to have gone unnoticed) is too complex a personage to enable one to point to a single model. He has many characteristics that reminded contemporaries of Anatole France, and Proust went so far as to plant real France sentences in passages of Bergotte's prose,[*] as if he had secretly wanted to sanction the identification. There are also undeniable traces of Ruskin in Bergotte's knowledge of medieval architecture, and a whiff of Pierre Loti in his disenchanted tone.

After the lunch is over, Bergotte and the Narrator leave together and strike up a long conversation: their shared passion for Racine and detestation of Norpois create an immediate bond of sympathy between them. A few days later, Swann's daughter, Gilberte, tells Marcel that he has charmed Bergotte, who declared him to be "very intelligent."

The acquaintance continues as the Narrator grows up, and he draws closer to Bergotte. He may be disappointed that the artist is so eager to ingratiate himself with society people and second-rate writers and journalists, and that he

---

[*] «vain songe de la vie», «tourment stérile et délicieux de comprendre et d'aimer», «émouvantes effigies qui anoblissent à jamais la façade vénérable et charmante des cathédrales». *1:95*, pointed out by Tadié, *Marcel Proust*, 725.

leads what appears to be such a boring life, but soon the young man comes to understand that it is not an interesting life that makes a great writer; rather, it is the ability to transform the elements of which a life is composed—whatever they may be—into something else: "But genius, and even great talent, springs less from seeds of intellect and social refinement superior to those of other people than from the faculty of transforming and transposing them. . . . Genius consist[s] in reflecting power and not in the intrinsic quality of the scene reflected."*

The older man builds up the Narrator's confidence by letting him talk, listening to him, and avoiding condescension when they disagree during their long conversations about books and the theater. And he urges the Narrator to write. Bergotte is very different from Anatole France in many respects, the most important distinction being his total lack of political engagement as opposed to France's very active role during the Dreyfus affair, but his relationship with the Narrator mirrors faithfully that between Proust and France. When he was still in school, Proust admired France with a passion that recalls the Narrator's at that age for Bergotte. Although he did not know him, he wrote Anatole France a veritable fan letter after reading a nasty review of one of his books: "I was so sorry to see you publicly belittled in this article that I am taking the liberty of writing to tell

---

* 1:537. *Mais le génie, même le grand talent, vient moins d'éléments intellectuels et d'affinement social supérieurs à ceux d'autrui, que de la faculté de les transformer, de les transposer . . . le génie consistant dans le pouvoir réfléchissant et non dans la qualité intrinsèque du spectacle reflété. 1:466.*

you how cruelly I resented it."* Later on Anatole France encouraged the young Proust, and wrote an introduction for his collection of essays, *Les plaisirs et les jours*. However, as the Narrator develops intellectually and emotionally, his admiration for Bergotte's work diminishes, even though he continues to read and reread his books. In real life, Proust's enthusiasm for France's writing also waned over the years. Nevertheless their friendship endured, strengthened by their common fight for Dreyfus, and Proust was so grateful to France for agreeing to sign a petition calling for judicial review of Dreyfus's court-martial conviction that he gave him a small Rubens drawing to thank him. However, in later years, when, as Anatole France put it, Proust had become neurasthenic and never left his bed, they stopped seeing each other, and France read Proust without any pleasure: "I've tried to understand him, and I haven't succeeded. It is not his fault, it's mine."[1] By that time, Proust had for many years outgrown his admiration, although he always remembered with gratitude France's many kindnesses. As in the case of Ruskin, he had reached a point at which he had to distance himself in order not to be "reduced to being no more than the full consciousness of another."†

Speaking for the Narrator, Proust points out that, after a year or two, he had absorbed Bergotte's thought and style completely, and that nothing in his work startled him anymore.

---

* My translation. *J'ai tant souffert de vous voir publiquement rapetissé dans cet article que j'ai pris la liberté de vous écrire quelle peine cruelle j'en ressentais.* Quoted by Chantal, *Marcel Proust*, 1:198.

† 4:463. *réduit à n'être que la pleine conscience d'un autre. 3:724.*

He had become so accustomed to the world unveiled by Bergotte that he could not remember the time when it had been impenetrable, and felt the need to turn to other authors for intellectual stimulation. Paradoxically, Bergotte, who has aged prematurely and suffers from a variety of illnesses, depends more and more on the Narrator for companionship and visits him regularly. He seems to enjoy these long hours with his young friend spent in a setting where he does not feel obliged to perform, as he still does in the salons of society ladies.

Thus their friendship thrives, although the Narrator admits being troubled by gossip about Bergotte's personal life. At this point, I sense a shift in the treatment of Bergotte: there is a growing confluence between Proust the writer and Bergotte the fictional character. It specifically concerns the apparent contradiction between the sensitivity exhibited in the writer's work and the callousness and perhaps even viciousness of his life. In the case of Bergotte, the reader will be told at the moment of his death that he seduced very young girls, and justified this vice with an absurd and amoral excuse: "'I spend more than a multi-millionaire on girls, but the pleasures or disappointments that they give me make me write a book which brings me in money.' . . . no doubt he found some charm in thus transmuting gold into caresses and caresses into gold."[*] Proust had an analogous problem: his taste for men that he insisted on concealing led to a double life. Some friends only knew the man who was famous for the delicacy

---

[*] 3:661. «Je dépense plus que des multimillionnaires pour des fillettes, mais les plaisirs et les déceptions qu'elles me donnent me font écrire un livre qui me rapporte de l'argent» . . . sans doute trouvait-il quelque agrément à transmuter ainsi l'or en caresses et les caresses en or. 3:154.

of his feelings, others knew someone more adventurous who was not averse to unusual sexual practices. Proust frequented male brothels and was known to like to witness, unobserved, certain activities. He was determined to keep that aspect of his life hidden and was extremely upset when his name was mentioned in a police report on such an establishment.

I turn to the real Proust here, because, as we have seen earlier, he never wore his homosexuality lightly and always tried to protect his privacy. Apparently even Jacques Rivière, his trusted editor, was in the dark about his sexual orientation. The only person in literary circles with whom Proust discussed it was André Gide, who was the star editor at Gallimard. By the 1920s, Proust was the publishing house's best-selling author, and the two men were on courteous, if not intimate, terms. Gide would come and chat with Proust in the late evenings. They faced the same predicament—how much should they allow to be known about their homosexuality?—but adopted different attitudes for dealing with it. Gide was cautious but, unlike Proust, not secretive about his tastes, and accused Proust of hypocrisy. It is worth noting, however, that Gide published *Corydon*, his treatise on homosexuality, only in 1924, whereas the first part of *Sodom and Gomorrah* appeared in 1921.

It is certain that Proust never stopped worrying about the effect his treatment of homosexuality would have on his readers. Given this preoccupation, I think it not unfair to read the following lines—ostensibly about Bergotte—as a reflection on his own life: "Perhaps it is only in really vicious lives that the problem of morality can arise in all its disquieting strength. And to this problem the artist offers a solution in the terms not of his own personal life but of what is for him his true life, a general, a literary solution. As the great Doctors of the Church began often, while remaining good, by experiencing the sins of all mankind, out of which they drew their own personal sanctity, so great artists often, while being wicked, make use of their vices in order to arrive at a conception of the moral law that is binding upon us all."* Would his readers turning the pages with acute discomfort arrive to the conclusion that all his literature was a lie and his sensitiveness mere playacting?

From this point on, Proust looks at Bergotte as though at his own reflection in a mirror. He inhabits the character he has created. It is not the Narrator who feels his way into Bergotte's mind, but Proust the man. The climax comes in *The Captive*: Bergotte has become ill; he sleeps very fitfully, suffers from recurrent, terrifying nightmares, "a sort of rehearsal . . . of the apoplectic stroke that was going to carry him off,"† and hardly leaves his home. This was Proust's own condition when he commenced work on the fifth volume of *La Recherche*, and he did not live to correct it to his satisfaction. Perhaps this is why, when Bergotte's death is described, a strange skid occurs: there is an inconsistency in the text. Ber-

---

* 1:541. *Peut-être n'est-ce que dans des vies réellement vicieuses que le problème moral peut se poser avec toute sa force d'anxiété. Et à ce problème l'artiste donne une solution non pas dans le plan de sa vie individuelle, mais de ce qui est pour lui sa vraie vie, une solution générale, littéraire. Comme les grands docteurs de l'Église commencèrent souvent tout en étant bons par connaître les péchés de tous les hommes, et en tirèrent leur sainteté personnelle, souvent les grands artistes tout en étant mauvais se servent de leurs vices pour arriver à concevoir la règle morale de tous. 1:469.*

† 3:662. *Une espèce de répétition . . . de l'attaque d'apoplexie qui allait l'emporter. 3:154.*

gotte was already famous when the Narrator was a young boy; we have seen the Narrator eager to meet the great man and thrilled by the present of Bergotte's slender volume on Racine. So it seems reasonable to suggest that, in the following passage in *The Captive*—which contradicts Bergotte's story as told in the earlier volumes—Proust is actually thinking of himself, to whom recognition as an incomparable writer came late in life, and who was still struggling hard to satisfy the demands of his publisher and his public at a time when he was terminally ill: "No doubt it often happens that only after his death does a writer become famous. But it was while he was still alive, and during his own slow progress towards approaching death, that this writer was able to watch the progress of his works towards Renown. A dead writer can at least be illustrious without any strain on himself. The effulgence of his name stops short at his gravestone. In the deafness of eternal sleep he is not importuned by Glory. But for Bergotte the antithesis was still incomplete. He existed still sufficiently to suffer from the tumult. He still moved about, though with difficulty, while his books, cavorting like daughters whom one loves but whose impetuous youthfulness and noisy pleasures tire one, brought day after day to his very bedside a crowd of fresh admirers."*

* 2:602. *Sans doute il arrive que c'est après sa mort seulement qu'un écrivain devient célèbre. Mais c'était en vie encore et durant son lent acheminement vers la mort non encore atteinte, qu'il assistait à celui de ses œuvres vers la Renommée. Un auteur mort est du moins illustre sans fatigue. Le rayonnement de son nom s'arrête à la pierre de sa tombe. Dans la surdité du sommeil éternel, il n'est pas importuné par la Gloire. Mais pour Bergotte l'antithèse n'était pas entièrement achevée. Il existait encore assez pour souffrir du tumulte. Il remuait encore, bien que péniblement, tandis que ses œuvres, bondissantes, comme des filles qu'on aime mais dont l'impétueuse jeunesse et les bruyants plaisirs vous fatiguent, entraînaient chaque jour jusqu'au pied de son lit des admirateurs nouveaux. 2:275.*

Exactly like his creator—who once very nearly died after drinking a wrong dose of laudanum—Bergotte distrusts his doctors, medicates himself, and tries different narcotics. "To what unknown forms of sleep, of dreams, is [the new drug] going to lead one? . . . Will it lead to illness? To blissful happiness? To death?"* Proust's visitors would easily recognize him in this description of the dying master:

Bergotte never went out of doors, and when he got out of bed for an hour in his room, he would be smothered in shawls, rugs, all the things with which a person covers himself before exposing himself to intense cold or going on a railway journey. He would apologise for them to the few friends whom he allowed to penetrate to his sanctuary; pointing to his tartan plaids, his travelling-rugs, he would say merrily: "After all, my dear fellow, life, as Anaxagoras has said, is a journey."†

When the time comes for Proust to arrange for Bergotte's death, he sends him to a Vermeer exhibition, where he has a fatal stroke. Bergotte, as he lies dying, obsessed by the beauty of the "little patch of yellow wall" which he has seen in one of the paintings, realizes that he should have written

* 3:664. *Vers quels genres ignorés de sommeil, de rêves [le produit nouveau] va-t-il nous conduire? . . . Nous mènera-t-il au malaise? A la béatitude? A la mort? 3:156.*

† 3:662. *Bergotte ne sortait plus de chez lui, et quand il se levait une heure dans sa chambre, c'était tout enveloppé de châles, de plaids, de tout ce dont on se couvre au moment de s'exposer à un grand froid ou de monter en chemin de fer. Il s'en excusait auprès des rares amis qu'il laissait pénétrer auprès de lui, et montrant ses tartans, ses couvertures, il disait gaiement: «Que voulez-vous, mon cher, Anaxagore l'a dit, la vie est un voyage.» 3:154.*

differently: "My last books are too dry, I ought to have gone over them with a few layers of colour, made my language precious in itself, like this little patch of yellow wall."*

In fact, Proust is describing what he himself had experienced in May 1921, when, making a huge effort, he went to the Jeu de Paume Museum to see the very same painting—*View of Delft*—before which Bergotte collapses. The difference is that Proust only suffered a frightening spell of giddiness. He was steadied by Jean-Louis Vaudoyer, a friend who accompanied him and led him out of the gallery. When Proust returned home, he asked his housekeeper, Céleste, for his manuscript of *The Captive*. "I have to add something to the death of Bergotte," he told her. In this manner, the real writer and the fictional one coalesce in the beautiful and exalting description of Bergotte's death. Of course Proust is not to be found exclusively in Bergotte; he is also present in the Narrator, the Narrator's Aunt Léonie, and Swann, as well as other, less important characters. But, to my mind, Bergotte has a special place, if only because, of all Proust's characters, he alone is certain to live on in his books:

He was dead. Dead for ever? Who can say? . . . [Was there not] a world entirely different from this one and which we leave in order to be born on this earth, before perhaps returning there to live once again . . . So that

---

* 3:665. *C'est ainsi que j'aurais dû écrire. Mes derniers livres sont trop secs, il aurait fallu passer quelques couches de couleur, rendre ma phrase en elle-même précieuse, comme ce petit pan de mur jaune.* 3:156.

the idea that Bergotte was not dead for ever is by no means improbable.

They buried him, but all through that night of mourning, in the lighted shop-windows, his books, arranged three by three, kept vigil like angels with outspread wings and seemed, for him who was no more, the symbol of his resurrection.[*]

[*] 3:665–66. *Il était mort. Mort à jamais? Qui peut le dire? [N'y a-t-il pas] un monde entièrement différent . . . dont nous sortons pour naître à cette terre, avant peut-être d'y retourner revivre . . . De sorte que l'idée que Bergotte n'était pas mort à jamais est sans invraisemblance. On l'enterra mais toute la nuit funèbre, aux vitrines éclairées, ses livres disposés trois par trois veillaient comme des anges aux ailes éployées et semblaient, pour celui qui n'était plus, le symbole de sa résurrection. 3:157.*

Conclusion...

There are as many ways to read as there are readers. But I believe that no one can read Proust without being captivated by the beauty and extreme originality of his style. He is the master of long sentences with a grammatical foundation so refined that they accommodate themselves miraculously to all the meanderings of his thoughts. Certainly, he is not to be speed read, but the consummate artist he is knows so well when to provide breaks and offer comic relief that the text surprises, challenges, and ultimately thrills the novice. Proust has created a prodigiously interwoven universe, the form and complexity of which do not reveal themselves easily; but fortunately, it is a universe within which are to be found planets—the worlds of the Guermantes, the Verdurins, and the Narrator's family, for example—inhabited by a diverse population of characters in turn moving, entertaining, hilarious, and cruel, to which readers are readily attracted. The same may be said of the complex world of literature that Proust himself inhabited.

An erudition as vast as Proust's necessarily reveals itself in his oeuvre through quotations, innuendoes, hints, and allusions overt or hidden. Discovering the alluvia that nourish and enrich his style adds much to the appreciation of his art. This is the reason I have endeavored to unveil the literary underpinning of his novel.

This book ends with the superb image of the afterlife of Bergotte's books because Proust's conviction of the permanence of great works of art gave him the inner strength necessary to pursue his work. Proust was painfully conscious of the vanity of love, friendship, success, and political passions. He described these emotions as fleeting, eaten away by social ambitions, jealousy, and selfishness. I am convinced that he would have been overwhelmed by despair if he had not believed so strongly in the beauty of nature and the significance of art. The delight he found in observing a flower, a riverbed, or the ever changing sea, the importance he ascribed to music, and even more so to painting—Vermeer represents the ideal that Bergotte, on his deathbed, regrets not having achieved—and, above all, to literature, proves it. It isn't enough that he names or quotes the great writers of the past: he has absorbed them; they are an integral part of his being, to the point of participating in its creation. As such their works will survive, not in the immutable way great monuments endure, but constantly rediscovered and reinterpreted thanks to Proust's unexpected, playful, and intensely personal take on different masterpieces. One of the great joys of reading *La Recherche* is to disentangle the rich and diverse contributions of the past.

Proust not only brought to the fore the beauty of centuries past but also set the scene for the era of modernism. This genius could not have so gloriously entered the twentieth century had he not proudly stood on the shoulders of giants.

Acknowledgments

Late in 2010, Jeannette Watson Sanger suggested we meet to talk about a Proust event she wanted to present at the New York Society Library. I was delighted at the prospect, and over a cup of tea we played with different ideas. None of them pleased us. Suddenly, Jeannette had an inspiration: How about Proust and books? After all, the event does take place in a library.

I gave the talk in April 2011. Helen Marx, with whom I had happily collaborated on other Proust projects, then proposed publishing an extended version of my talk. Very sadly, she did not live to see the completion of the project. Jonathan Rabinowitz then stepped in and offered a home to my manuscript. When Judith Gurewich, the publisher of Other Press, expressed her interest in publishing it, he very graciously agreed to hand it over to her.

Many thanks to Sophia Sherry, who showed endless patience and relentless precision in the preparation of the manuscript; to Marjorie DeWitt and Sulay Hernandez, whose comments on the text were invaluable; and to Yvonne E. Cárdenas and Iisha Stevens, who, with great resolve and dedication, turned the manuscript into a book. I have been very fortunate in having Judith Gurewich as both my editor and my publisher: her sharp questions and shrewd suggestions led me to develop many aspects of the book and reexamine rigorously some of my views. My gratitude to her and to my husband, Louis Begley, who read, reread, and read yet again, is endless.

Permissions Acknowledgments

Grateful acknowledgment is made for permission to reproduce selections from the following:

In Search Of Lost Time, Vol. 1: Swann's Way; Within A Budding Grove (Part One); In Search Of Lost Time, Vol. 2: Within A Budding Grove (Part Two); The Guermantes Way; In Search Of Lost Time, Vol. 3: Sodom And Gomorrah; The Captive; and In Search Of Lost Time, Vol. 4: The Fugitive; Time Regained by Marcel Proust, revised by D.J. Enright, translated by C.K. Moncrieff and Terence Kilmartin, translation copyright © 1981 by Chatto & Windus and Random House, Inc. Revisions to the translation copyright © 1992 by D. J. Enright. Used by permission of Modern Library, a division of Random House, Inc.

In Search of Lost Time by Marcel Proust. Published by Chatto & Windus. Reprinted by permission of The Random House Group Limited UK.

By Way of Sainte-Beuve by Marcel Proust, translated by Sylvia Townsend Warner, published by Chatto & Windus. Reprinted by permission of The Random House Group Limited.

Les Fleurs du Mal by Charles Baudelaire. Translated from the French by Richard Howard. Reprinted by permission of David R. Godine, Publisher, Inc. Translation copyright © 1982 by Richard Howard.

Notes

I. First Impressions and Lasting Influences

1. My translation. Proust, *Jean Santeuil* (Paris: Gallimard, 1952), 1:178–79.
2. The magic lantern, ancestor of the modern slide projector, allowed the projection of a still image on a wall.
3. Saint-Simon, *Mémoires* (Paris: Gallimard, la Pléiade, 1987), 7:399. Saint-Simon means that he feels free to disregard the dictates of the Académie Française.
4. Geneviève Straus was the daughter of the composer Fromenthal Halévy and the widow of Georges Bizet. She presided over one of the intellectual and political salons of the time. Extremely witty, she provided Proust with some of the funniest repartees of the Duchess de Guermantes, a main character in his novel.
5. François-René de Chateaubriand, *Mémoires d'Outre-tombe* (Paris: Gallimard, 1971), 3:1, quoted by Proust in 4:488, *3:744*.
6. My translation. Proust, *Lettres*, 320.
7. Adriana Hunter's translation. Proust, *Carnets*, quoted by Bernard de Fallois in Proust, *Contre Sainte-Beuve* (Paris: Gallimard, 1954), Préface, 35.
8. *Swann's Way* was rejected by Gallimard and by two other publishers, Ollendorf and Fasquelle. Grasset agreed to publish the novel in 1912 but Proust paid the expenses. Publication was suspended during the First World War; Grasset closed temporarily and Proust then moved to Gallimard.
9. Marcel Proust to Robert de Billy, n.d., in Proust, *Letters of Marcel Proust*, 245.

II. Foreign Incursions

1. Quoted by Jean-Yves Tadié, *Marcel Proust: A Life*, trans. Euan Cameron (New York: Viking, 2000), 346.

2. Richard Macksey, "'Conclusions' et 'Incitations': Proust à la recherche de Ruskin," *MLN* 96, No. 5 (December 1981): 113–119.

3. Proust, *On Reading Ruskin: Prefaces to "La Bible d'Amiens" and "Sésame et les Lys,"* trans. and ed. Jean Autret, William Burford, and Phillip J. Wolfe (New Haven, CT: Yale University Press, 1987), xx.

4. Ibid., 145–46.

5. Adriana Hunter's translation. Proust, *Contre Sainte-Beuve* (1971), 104.

6. My translation. Marcel Proust to Mme Mandrazo, quoted in Tadié, *Proust et le roman* (Paris: Gallimard, 2003), 95.

7. Adriana Hunter's translation. Proust, *Contre Sainte-Beuve* (1971), 640.

8. Marcel Proust to Robert de Billy, n.d., in *Letters of Marcel Proust*, 245. For "admirable geometrical parallelism": Nouvelles Acquisitions Françaises (Bibliothèque Nationale, 16637 48r.), quoted by Emily Eells, *Proust's Cup of Tea: Homoeroticism and Victorian Culture* (Surrey, UK: Ashgate, 2002), 68.

9. Carnet 1, Nouvelles Acquisitions Françaises (Bibliothèque Nationale, 16637 35 r.), quoted by Eells, *Proust's Cup of Tea*, 82–83.

10. Quoted in A. S. Byatt's introduction to George Eliot, *The Mill on the Floss* (New York: Penguin Classics, 2003), xviii, xxiv, xxxii.

11. *Jean Santeuil*, quoted in Eells, *Proust's Cup of Tea*, 85.

III. Good Readers and Bad Readers

1. Corneille, *Horace*, act 1, scene 2: If you are not a Roman, be worthy of one.

2. My translation. Lettre à Jacques Rivière, n.d., in Proust, *Marcel Proust et Jacques Rivière: Correspondance 1914–1922* (Paris: Plon, 1955).

3. The Concours Général is a national competition held every year among students of the *Première* (eleventh grade) and the *Terminale* (twelfth and final grade) in almost all subjects taught in both general, technological, and professional high schools. One or two students per class are chosen to compete by their teachers.

4. Proust quoted a line of Vigny's as an epigraph of *Sodom and Gomorrah*: *La femme aura Gomorrhe et l'homme aura Sodome*, and cited another one in his portrait of the homosexual: *Les deux sexes mourront chacun de leur côté*.

5. The Dreyfus affair was a political and judicial scandal that tore France apart in the 1890s and the early 1900s. It involved the wrongful conviction for treason in December 1894 of Captain Alfred Dreyfus, a Jewish officer in the French Army. Sentenced to life imprisonment for allegedly having sold French military secrets to the German military attaché in Paris, Dreyfus was sent to the penal colony at Devil's Island in French Guiana, where he was held for almost five years in solitary confinement. Eventually, all the accusations were shown to have been baseless, and Dreyfus was exonerated.

IV. A Homosexual Reader: Baron de Charlus

1. Cited without reference in Jacques Borel, *Proust et Balzac* (Paris: Corti, 1975), 13.

2. James McNeill Whistler, *Arrangement in Black and Gold: Comte Robert de Montesquiou-Fézensac* (1891), the Frick Collection, New York City.

V. Racine: A Second Language

1. *Phèdre*, act 1, scene 3. "What efficious hand/Has tied these knots, and gather'd o'er my brow/These clustering coils?" Racine, *Phaedra*, trans. R. B. Boswell.

VI. The Goncourts

1. Marcel Proust to Robert de Montesquiou, n.d., in *Letters of Marcel Proust*, 437.

VII. Bergotte: The Writer in the Novel

1. M. Le Goff, *Anatole France à la Béchellerie* (Albin Michel), 331, quoted by Tadié, *Marcel Proust*, 725.

bibliography

Marcel Proust

À la recherche du temps perdu. 3 vols. Paris: Robert Laffont/Quid, 1987.

By Way of Sainte-Beuve. Translated by Sylvia Townsend Warner. London: Chatto and Windus, 1958.

Contre Sainte-Beuve, précédé de Pastiches et mélanges et suivi de Essais et articles. Paris: Gallimard, Bibliothèque de la Pléiade, 1971.

Contre Sainte-Beuve, suivi de Nouveaux mélanges. Préface de Bernard de Fallois. Paris: Gallimard, 1954.

Correspondance. Edited by Philip Kolb. 21 vols. Paris: Éditions Plon, 1970–93.

Correspondance Générale. Paris: Gallimard, 1976.

Days of Reading. Translated by John Sturrock. New York: Penguin Books, 2008.

In Search of Lost Time. Translated by C. K. Scott Moncrieff and Terence Kilmartin. Revised by D. J. Enright with an Introduction by Harold Bloom. 4 vols. New York: Everyman's Library, distributed by Random House, 2001.

Jean Santeuil. 3 vols. Paris: Gallimard, 1952.

Letters of Marcel Proust. Translated by Mina Curtiss. New York: Helen Marx Books and Books and Co., imprints of Turtle Point Press, 2006.

Lettres. Paris: Éditions Plon, 2004.

Lettres à Reynaldo Hahn. Paris: Gallimard, 1956.

Marcel Proust et Jacques Rivière: Correspondance 1914–1922. Paris: Éditions Plon, 1955.

On Reading Ruskin: Prefaces to "La Bible d'Amiens" and "Sésame et les Lys." Translated and edited by Jean Autret, William Burford, and Phillip J. Wolfe. Introduction by Richard Macksey. New Haven, CT: Yale University Press, 1987.

Sur la Lecture. Paris: Actes Sud, 1988.

Baudelaire, Charles. *Les Fleurs du Mal.* Translated by Richard Howard. Boston: David R. Godine, 1983.

———. *Œuvres complètes.* 2 vols. Paris: Gallimard, Bibliothèque de la Pléiade, 1975–76.

Borel, Jacques. *Proust et Balzac.* Paris: Librairie José Corti, 1975.

Bouillaguet, Annick. *Proust et les Goncourt: Le pastiche du "Journal" dans "Le Temps retrouvé."* Paris: Archives des Lettres Modernes, 1996.

Chantal, René de. *Marcel Proust, critique littéraire.* 2 vols. Montréal: Presses de l'Université de Montréal, 1967.

Chateaubriand, François-René de. *Mémoires d'outre-tombe.* Paris: Gallimard, Bibliothèque de la Pléiade, 1971.

Compagnon, Antoine. *Proust Between Two Centuries.* New York: Columbia University Press, 1992.

Eells, Emily. *Proust's Cup of Tea: Homoeroticism and Victorian Culture.* Surrey, UK: Ashgate, 2002.

Eliot, George. *The Mill on the Floss.* Introduction by A. S. Byatt. New York: Penguin Classics, 2003.

Ferré, André. *Les Années de Collège de Marcel Proust.* Paris: Gallimard, 1959.

Gide, André. *Journal 1887–1925.* Paris: Gallimard, Bibliothèque de la Pléiade, 1996.

———. *Journals.* Translated by Justin O'Brien. 4 vols. New York: Alfred A. Knopf, 1948.

Goncourt, Edmond de, and Jules de Goncourt. *Journal.* 3 vols. Paris: Robert Laffont, 1956.

Levaillant, Jean. "Notes sur le personnage de Bergotte." *Revue des sciences humaines,* January–March, 1952.

Levin, Harry. "Balzac et Proust." In *Hommage à Balzac.* (UNESCO). Paris: Mercure de France, 1950.

Macksey, Richard. "'Conclusions' et 'Incitations': Proust à la recherche de Ruskin." *MLN* 96, no. 5 (December 1981): 113–19.

Mouton, Jean. *Le Style de Marcel Proust.* Paris: Éditions Corrêa, 1948.

Racine, Jean. *Esther,* in *Esther and Berenice: Two Plays.* Translated by John Masefield. New York: Macmillan, 1922.

———. *Phaedra,* in *The Dramatic Works of Jean Racine, Vol. I.* Translated by Robert Bruce Boswell. London: George Bell and Sons, 1908. Gutenberg eBook, 2008.

Saint-Simon, Duke de. *Mémoires*. 8 vols. Paris: Gallimard, Bibliothèque de la Pléiade, 1983–88.

Tadié, Jean-Yves. *Proust et le roman*. Paris: Gallimard, 2003.

———. *Marcel Proust: A Life*. Translated by Euan Cameron. New York: Viking, 2000.

Vigny, Alfred de. *Œuvres poétiques*. Paris: Garnier-Flammarion, 1978.

A Note About the Illustrations

I could not have hoped for a more Proustian illustrator than Andreas Gurewich. His collaboration with Gary Roar led to deft, humoristic drawings whose complex meaning, both literal and abstract, match and illuminate the text. For instance, the scaffolding that introduces the chapter on Ruskin symbolizes at once the ladder on which Proust climbed up to study Venetian capitals, the layers of texts necessary for a full reading of *La Recherche* and its intricate architecture. On the endpapers, the imaginary tombstone with the name *Marcel* masked by a garland of hawthorns echoes Proust's reflection on books being cemeteries in which one can hardly read the writing on the monuments. And how fitting a conclusion than that of the little bird dipping a madeleine into a cup of tea, which evokes the inspiration Proust drew from Chateaubriand for the most famous page of his novel, in the most precise and charming manner. My warmest thanks to both of them.